Plea[se]

Pastor Cheryl Mark

403 7032743

DEVELOPING A PROSPEROUS SOUL

VOLUME II

HOW TO MOVE INTO
GOD'S FINANCIAL BLESSINGS

HAROLD R. EBERLE

 Winepress Publishing
Yakima, Washington

Developing a Prosperous Soul, Vol. II
How to Move into God's Financial Blessings

© 1997 by Harold R. Eberle
First Printing, July 1997
Second Printing, March 2001

Winepress Publishing
P.O. Box 10653
Yakima, WA 98909-1653
(509) 248-5837
www.winepress.org
winepress@nwinfo.net

Library of Congress Control No. 97-060375
ISBN 1-882523-06-7
Cover design by Gerrit Dieleman

Unless otherwise stated, all biblical quotations are taken from the New American Standard Bible © 1977, The Lockman Foundation, La Habra, California 90631.

Printed in the United States of America

Table of Contents

Introduction

This is not a how-to-get-rich book. Rather, it explains how to prosper. Prosperity is better! It is living in God's abundance, God's way.

In Volume I we laid out key principles concerning the development of a sense of dominion. We learned what it means to "seek first the kingdom of God" and, hence, release "God's adding power" into our lives. We also introduced several terms related to changing how we think. For example, when we talk about *poverty-minded,* we are describing a way of thinking which produces defeat. In contrast, when we refer to *prosperous attitudes* or *prosperous ways of thinking,* we are explaining the attitudes and thought patterns which lead to success in life. We examined the differences in lifestyles between successful individuals and people who always seem to be struggling. Our goal is to develop prosperous attitudes which will produce abundance in our lives.

Volume II will contrast further poverty thinking and prosperity thinking; however, we also will explain *what to do*...not only how to think, but steps you actually can take to break poverty's hold and receive the abundance God wants for your life.

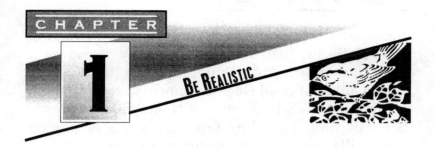

CHAPTER

1

BE REALISTIC

Poverty-minded people tend to look for the big break, the miraculous provision, the chance deal. Prosperous people know good things will happen along life's path, but they expect steady progress through their own consistent, diligent work.

That's why poor people buy lottery tickets. Just stop where lottery tickets are sold and observe who purchases the vast majority of them. Wealthy individuals know a lottery ticket is a very bad investment. The odds of winning are minuscule, so purchasing one is like throwing away money. The government which backs the sale of lottery tickets knows that it is simply an alternative to taxing the poor. The poor buy the tickets, so the poor lose their money. They often feel helpless to escape their present circumstances, so they look to chance, rather than consistent work, as the answer to their problems.

This lottery mentality sometime is embraced by Christians and incorporated into their belief system. Some Christians will tell you about one miraculous provision after another. They have dozens of testimonies about God rescuing them from some financial dilemmas—yet they still are struggling financially in their daily lives. It may sound as if they have much faith; but in reality, if they did, they would not need God constantly to rescue them. If you take a realistic view of their life, you probably will find that they typically are late paying their bills, and that their financial life is up and down like a roller coaster. They simply have replaced the lottery ticket with "God."

Of course, God does provide. However, Christians, more than any other people, should know advancement comes first to those who apply God's principles on a consistent, long-term basis. The Bible tells us to be "...*imitators of those who through faith and patience inherit the promises*" (Heb. 6:12). At the foundation of God's principles are hard work, wisdom, and consistency. Good, even amazing, things do happen to people in motion.

Many poverty-minded people never embrace this. Deep down, they think success is out of reach, happening to some and not to others. They are helpless, paralyzed to some degree, because their eyes are set on the chance that may come, rather than today's step forward.

When they see people prospering around them, they often hold deep suspicions that those who are already rich succeeded not through hard work, but rather through some extra boost along life's way, such as a large inheritance, major legal settlement, gift from Uncle George, or dishonest dealings. While some people do receive such benefits during their lifetime, the vast majority of those who win a lottery or receive unearned money lose it in a very short time. People who do earn wealth and keep it, do so because they are *realists* when it comes to money.

Let's talk about being realists concerning your present situation in life. Many people have unrealistic financial expectations that put constant stress upon them and their relationships with those they love.

For example, young newlyweds just starting out in life are likely to have financial struggles. They probably will not be living in a new home, and when their first baby comes along, they may be very surprised to discover how little extra money they have for themselves.

Most Americans in their thirties have finished their schooling and are settling into a career. If they have a family, their children will be in school. If they own or rent a home, they will start taking better care of their lawn and investing in nicer furniture. It is a time of becoming established and more stable.

People in their forties typically are thinking about college expenses for their children, retirement, and longer-term investments. Those in their forties usually are able to move from just paying the bills to setting aside some money for the future.

Those in their fifties generally find it easier to make money than at any other time in their life. Their years of experience, developing relationships, and accumulating knowledge bring greater opportunities, and they usually can accomplish tasks with much less time and effort.

Of course, there are numerous exceptions to the above scenarios. People experience changes and upheavals. Each has his own unique situation and problems with which to deal.

Our objective, however, is to help people achieve realistic expectations of their financial situations. Newlyweds should not expect to own the same quality automobile as people in their forties. If a 30-year-old constantly is comparing his own financial position with his parents', he is putting undue stress upon himself. Comparing yourself with anyone in less difficult circumstances is foolish.

Reality is what we are after here.

Realistic thinking is often more difficult for Christians than non-Christians. For example, a Christian struggling financially may analyze himself constantly, wondering if he has offended God, or if the devil is harassing him. Hence, he does not know whether to fight the devil or repent before God; when in reality, financial difficulties are most often the result of spending too much money or not earning enough. Reality is simple. Christians sometime make it complicated in their desperate desire to please God. Usually, the best way to help them is tell them to set aside all spiritual issues, and for a moment think in terms of natural reality. Ask, "Why don't you have enough money?" As you ask this, do not allow them to flip into a spiritual answer involving God or the devil. Just keep things simple. Reality is truth, and whether we are dealing with God or the devil, truth is the solution.

Here is truth: a physician typically makes more money than a carpenter. The carpenter does not make less money because he has offended God or the devil is against him. He makes less money because he makes less money.

It is surprising how many people cannot face such obvious truth when they themselves are struggling financially. I talk with many ministers and sometime meet one who is unable to support his family. When I ask him why, he may respond with all kinds of spiritual-sounding answers. In reality, those who cannot support their families usually cannot do so because they are not making enough money—it's that simple. The minister's church is too small to pay him enough, or he just started in ministry, or he is doing something foolish financially. It is not God or the devil. It is life.

Chapter 3 deals with choosing a career and whether or not a person already working should change careers. In other chapters, we will explain how people can improve their financial situation no matter what their current income. This chapter is to help people become realists.

Most adults who read this book already will have found a job and have established circumstances around them which fix their lifestyle to some degree.

If you are a homemaker with children and you know God wants you there, then that is your present career. Don't feel badly about it. Accept it. Enjoy it. Be the best Mom or Dad you can be.

If you are a carpenter and you enjoy your work, then go on enjoying it. Don't change. Some people enjoy manual labor, while others enjoy sales or management or some other area of employment. The key is to do what you enjoy and feel good about it.

King Solomon, who had wisdom from God, wrote:

> *There is nothing better for a man than*
> *to eat and drink and tell himself that*
> *his labor is good.*　　　　(Eccl. 2:24a)

Nothing better! Nothing better than to enjoy life and feel good about what you are doing! This is more important than a high-paying, high-pressure position and more beneficial to your long-term health than a good diet or exercise. God desires you to enjoy life; so if you have a career or position which you feel is in God's will, then embrace it and be content there, even if you are not getting rich.

Remember, this is not about getting rich, it is about developing a prosperous soul. The theme of this book is taken from the Apostle John's prayer:

> *Beloved, I pray that in all respects you*
> *may prosper and be in good health,*
> *just as your soul prospers.*
> 　　　　　　(III John vs. 2)

Notice that health and prosperity are the natural outworkings of a prosperous soul. Prosperity is not necessarily being wealthy. Prosperity is an attitude. It is health of soul. If the inside is healthy, the outside will be also.

Therefore, if you are in a low-paying employment situation, decide if that is where God wants you. If you are happy there, and if you are convinced that God wants you where you are, then be at peace. Stop worrying. Stay there.

But at the same time, don't deceive yourself into believing that someday you will be rich. There are certain things you can do to increase your financial position no matter what your income is, and we will discuss those. But here we are laying down a fundamental principle: *At the center of having a prosperous soul is finding contentment in what you do.* You do not have to be rich to be prosperous, but you do have to be realistic. This does not mean you must accept defeat or poverty as a way of life. On the contrary, cultivating prosperity of soul will help you succeed in all areas of life.

Think again about your career or present situation of life. If you are where God wants you, then accept it. Stop putting yourself under undue pressure. More importantly, don't carry a bad attitude around with you—that flows over onto everyone else. If you feel badly about your job, you are going to bring that attitude home with you and grumble to your spouse and children. Whatever stress you put upon yourself, you are going to put on your loved ones, too. No one needs that. So face reality; if you are where God wants you, stop worrying.

9

Similarly, if there are circumstances limiting your advancement, accept reality. Consider Bob who was injured severely in a car accident. Bob always had wanted to be a professional baseball player, but he lost both of his legs. He can go on living in a myth that someday he will play pro ball, or he can accept his present limitations and do the best with what he has. If Bob lives in a dream world, he will waste days, weeks, months, and years in emotional turmoil, one day fantasizing about a moment on the field, the next hating himself for his handicap. Depression and discouragement will overwhelm him for as long as he denies reality and lives in an illusion. In addition, friends and family will suffer as they feel his agony and share his disillusionment. On the other hand, if Bob accepts reality, he can find fulfillment and happiness.

Your situation is not likely to be so limiting, but you may be locked into a position for some time to come. Accept reality. Stop dreaming about becoming something you won't become or won't become quickly. That only causes pain for you and others.

If you enjoy working with your hands and feel God wants you doing that, stop feeling guilty. Stop feeling badly about the older car you drive. You may not be able to live up to the lifestyles of your parents, friends, or neighbors. Who cares? Stop trying to keep up with the Jones.

If you are locked into a fixed retirement income or taking care of your elderly parent, and that is limiting your lifestyle for years ahead, stop putting pressure on yourself to change. Accept it. You may not be able to give a thousand dollars to your grandchild for his graduation. You probably won't go on the cruise to the Caribbean with the senior citizens. That's life!

If you are a mother who needs to be at home taking care of your precious little ones for the next few years, enjoy it. Stop gazing at the single, care-free 20-year-old driving her hot red sports car. It's not you. And stop longing for a high-powered ca-reer. It won't happen, at least not for a few years, so why beat yourself up all the time?

Maybe you have committed yourself to work at your father's business for the next few years, and there is no way out of that commitment. Maybe you are a minister and you know God has called you to work among the poor and needy. Or perhaps you are in some other situation that simply cannot be changed.

It is OK to be where you are. Let reality com-pletely murder false dreams.

If you have several thousand dollars' worth of medical bills ahead of you, guess what? You are not going to Hawaii on vacation this year! That's real-ity! If you are paying for your child's college educa-tion, you may not be able to buy a boat like the guy next door. So what? Who cares? I don't. No one is putting pressure on you but you. Accept reality. It's easier.

These issues are important. You cannot be happy in life until you settle them. Answer the following question by checking Yes or No:

Am I where God wants me? ___ Yes ___ No

If you checked "Yes," you need to relax and enjoy life. In fact, if that is true, I suggest that you skip the next two chapters and continue reading at chapter four. If you checked "No," you need to read the next two chapters and consider changing your career.

If you cannot check either of the above, your soul is not healthy. Every time someone drives by in their luxury sedan, you will experience longings to have what they have. Every time your in-laws glance at you with that why-aren't-you-doing-better-financially look in their eyes, you will feel pain inside. Every time you watch a television show and see people more financially blessed than you, you will wrestle inside wondering why you are not so blessed.

You cannot be at peace unless you know you are where God wants you. If you are there, stop putting pressure on yourself. Knock it off! If you are not where God wants you, read on.

From our theme verse, III John verse 2, we can learn that God desires us to prosper and be in health, even as our soul prospers. What I would like you next to realize from this verse is the *directional lifestyle toward abundance.* Advancing! The prosperous person sees life as a road constantly increasing in God's grace and blessings. In contrast, the poverty-minded person feels stuck and has accepted this as what life should be.

As we talk about this distinction, at first it may sound contradictory to what we taught in the last chapter about accepting your present position, if you know that is where God wants you. Please, do not be confused here. In the previous chapter, we were explaining a restful attitude of heart, which produces prosperity. The prosperous soul is at peace; however, it continues to expect God's blessings. *It is not striving for those blessings, but it rests in reality, knowing that God will abundantly provide.*

When we contrast the advancing mind-set with the trapped mind-set, we see that each produces different results in people's lives. Before we discuss some of them, identify clearly the distinction we are emphasizing here.

The prosperous soul has vision, hope, and direction. A person's current financial position does not matter if they have a prosperous soul. They will be productive and putting out energy.

Consider Kay, a Christian lady who went through a terrible financial crisis, but who, because of a prosperous attitude, continued to move ahead in hope and confidence. One day Kay discovered that she did not have enough food in her kitchen to pack a regular lunch to send with her children to school. That did not discourage nor stop her from being productive and creative. She instantly shifted gears to solve the problem. That one morning she found enough ingredients to bake cupcakes. She immediately got busy and baked a fresh batch. Then she sat her children down and taught each of them how to take out those cupcakes at lunch time and trade them with other children in the school cafeteria for more nutritious food items. They ate like kings, plus they learned skills in salesmanship.

Another parent in Kay's predicament, lacking a prosperous outlook, would have gone into confusion and despair. They would have felt abandoned and lost—even paralyzed.

One reason Kay or any prosperous person does succeed is because they already have oriented their life in a specific direction: toward success! Kay was not going to accept defeat. This is a key. Kay did not have to wrestle with fears and doubts. She needed to succeed; her children needed to eat. There was no question in her mind but to advance.

14

We cannot emphasize enough this characteristic of the prosperous soul. Motivational energy from within a person is first and foremost determined by that person's ability to know where they are headed. Jesus said, *"...if your eye is clear, your whole body will be full of light"* (Matt. 6:22b). If you have a clear focus concerning what you need to do in life, you will find spiritual energy arising within you that will help you succeed. When a person does not know where he is headed or has too many options, he tends to go into confusion. His mind goes blank.

Kay had the key issue settled for the care of her children. She needed to go ahead. I am asking you to settle this for the orientation of your life: Does God want you to advance?

Christians more often are confused over this than non-Christians. When a new job opportunity stands before them, they must think through all the advantages and disadvantages. In addition, the Christian desiring to please God may wrestle with dozens of questions such as: "Will this be good for my Christian witness?" "Will I be bound together with unbelievers?" "Will I be unfair to my present boss if I leave him?" "Is this my flesh pushing me to success?" "Does God want me to have this job?" and "Is the devil opening up this position?" Such questions can seem endless.

The important point is that a multitude of questions can paralyze a person. Compare this with the lion tamer working at a circus with his big cats. It is common for lion tamers to carry a chair with them and push it in front of the lions' faces. Why? Because lions will attack only if they can focus on one object. When the legs of the chair are moving in front of them, they go into confusion. People are like that, too. *Motivational energy from within a person is first and foremost determined by that person's ability to know where they are headed.* The Bible declares that a double-minded person should not expect to receive God's help (James 1:7-8). That verse was written to Christians. The Christian who cannot determine where he is headed will not have God's power working with him. It is that simple.

Now, we are not telling Christians to throw out all their questions and considerations concerning how a potential job will affect their spiritual and natural welfare. No. What we are doing here is trying to get you to embrace an orientation toward success. God wants you to advance. It is His will.

Embracing this orientation will make your decisions much easier. You will find stronger motivational energy arising from within you. Creative energy will flow. As in Kay's situation, you will shift gears easier and continue toward the goal of advancement. Every problem you face will be converted into an opportunity. Your eyes will be open to see possibilities you never saw before. When a person's orientation is right and clear, God helps them succeed.

The desire to advance is right, healthy, and good. After God created Adam and Eve, He blessed them saying, *"Be fruitful and multiply, and fill the earth, and subdue it"* (Gen. 1:28). This was part of God's blessings. It is a good thing. At that point, God instilled in the nature of mankind the desire to be fruitful. Therefore, Christians with a healthy desire to advance and be fruitful should not feel guilty. In fact, they need to realize this is exactly what God wants for their lives.

In the book of Isaiah, we read the words of God speaking to us:

> *"I am the Lord your God, <u>who</u> <u>teaches</u>*
> *<u>you</u> <u>to</u> <u>profit,</u>*
> *Who leads you in the way you should*
> *go."* (Is. 48:17b; emphasis added)

It is God who wants you to profit. Further, Deuteronomy 8:18 tells us that it is God who gives us the *"power to make wealth."* God teaches us to profit and He gives us power to do so. Obviously, He wants us to advance!

Yet, many Christians feel guilty about prospering. They are afraid to make a profit, <u>not realizing they are resisting the leading and empowering of God</u>. Don't do that! Let God bless you. Go in the direction He wants to lead you—ahead, to make a profit, to advance.

Married couples often encounter difficulties on this point. One individual in the relationship may be more eager to advance than his or her spouse, sometime leading to frustration and discouragement. Often one gives up on the other or tries to go ahead without spousal support, sometime causing marital tension. No amount of financial success is worth losing one's spouse. Reading this book may add to the faith and energy of the partner more determined to advance. I caution you, though, in a good marriage *two stay one*, united in heart and purpose. Often the more energetic person will have to "die" to their own passion and desire to succeed. One's spouse always must be held in higher regard than success. Do not be confused about this. Communicate from your heart often and exalt your mate in your heart above your own desire to succeed, and gradually he/she may catch your vision. Even if he/she does not, success in material things is not worth the loss of your beloved.

Another caution pertains to biblical warnings about greed, lust for money, anxiousness, and striving to get ahead quickly. We are warned that get-rich-quick schemes lead to ruin (Prov. 28:20b). The Apostle Paul writes to his disciple Timothy that those who fill their life with longings to get rich will fall into many temptations and destruction (I Tim. 6:9). We must heed these warnings.

However, we also need a healthy attitude about being fruitful and productive in life. It is frustrating for a father to work year after year and never get ahead. It is hard to labor at the same job faithfully without ever receiving a promotion. It is not right. And, in fact, it should not be accepted. A Christian should expect God to bless them as they continue working faithfully with a prosperous attitude. It is this step-by-step, gradual advancement that we are encouraging.

Years ago while pastoring, I had a poverty mind-set regarding church growth. I felt stuck with a small church and at the same time I continued longing for some sudden, amazing growth to happen in the size of my congregation. I wanted my small congregation to explode in size overnight, but it never happened. Then one day I heard a very successful minister say, "Sonny, no one's gonna' hand ya' a church; if ya' want a ministry, yer' gonna' have to build it!" That day I began building instead of waiting around for someone (or Someone) to hand me a ministry. I decided to get unstuck. I started building into the people I already had. Every week I built on what I had established the week before, and I determined that I would do this over the long haul. When I changed my attitude, the church began to grow.

This is how God works. If you want to prosper, then orient your life toward success and start building right where you are. It does not matter how much you presently own. We are teaching a lifestyle, one that will lead to success and blessings from God.

Here is how it works in real life: the person working 8 to 5 will do his very best for his employer. He gives more than he is given. He shows up for work on time and stays until the work is done. He does the best he can do and puts his heart into his work (Col. 3:23). At the same time, he believes that God will prosper him for his faithfulness.

The self-employed person is not looking for overnight success, but determines to build his clientele over many years. He wants to serve his customers, providing a service or product at a fair, honest price. He expects to succeed because he is doing his best.

When prosperous individuals find themselves without employment and financially devastated, they keep their energy flowing: wearing clean clothes, fixing their hair, cleaning their car, meeting people and working as soon as possible, even at a minimum wage job. Out there where they are active, they soon will see the opportunities to advance to a job which is better, and better, and so on.

Progress—raises, promotions, and God's blessings—is expected, but faithfulness and steady progress are the path.

The poverty mind-set, on the other hand, dictates that a person wait for the big break to come along. Confusion hits the mind. Sleepiness lingers over their eyes. The poverty mentality causes them to wait and wait. While they are waiting, they inwardly grumble because present circumstances are difficult. They tend to think that life is not fair, concluding that it's more difficult for them than for anyone else.

Millions of people are living inactively on government-aid programs. There is nothing wrong with using government aid if and when it is used as a helping step toward advancement. The poverty mind, however, receives other people's help while "turning the motion button off." They passively wait for the perfect job. They are unwilling to accept low-paying work because they think it will hinder them from getting "the big break" that may come along. They sit motionless, not realizing that it is their poverty mind-set that keeps them in prison.

One day I offered work to a man holding a sign saying, "Will work for food." I promised him well over the minimum wage. When he heard my offer, he scoffed, saying he was worth a lot more than that. I drove off knowing why he was unemployed.

A prosperous soul will begin wherever it is and work toward advancement. A poverty mind-set is looking for a handout. Sonny, no one is gonna' hand you prosperity! If ya' want it, ya' gotta' build it—at a steady, consistent pace. That is how God works.

It is now time to talk to everyone considering a change in their employment. If you are happy in your present employment, then skip this chapter. If, however, you are not satisfied, there is something you can do. You can change.

Changing careers is not as difficult as it may seem. A career counselor told me the statistic that the average American changes jobs 24 times and careers four times during his/her life. You can do it, too. In fact you ought to expect it.

The world in which you live is changing rapidly. We no longer live in a society where people can go to work and settle into one company for their entire life. Those days are over. The person who wants to find the perfect job and get comfortable is in for a rude awakening. Change is in the air. To thrive in our culture you always should look for new opportunities, learn a new trade, take a training course, develop a new skill, learn more about computers, accept a new challenge, grow in your field, etc. A man I respect who travels worldwide once said, "I think I have at least six more languages to learn." He was over 60 years old at the time. In days gone by, people thought in terms of learning a trade in their twenties, then coasting in that employment field for the rest of their days. Today, that road leads to poverty.

Unfortunately, some people find it hard to change. They grumble daily about their present circumstances, but it never dawns on them that they actually can do something about it. Then one day they get sick and tired of being sick and tired. They finally get so fed up with being poor, unable to pay their bills, and weary of their work environment that they break free. Sometime in those radical escapes they burn their bridges and, hence, suffer tremendously while trying to re-establish themselves in a new career.

You do not have to wait until your day of explosion. Maybe you are already there. How much better, though, to make career decisions for your future while you have a level head. Do not quit your job today. Keep working, but today start making plans so that a year or two from now you can be doing something else. That is the way to approach this issue: decide where you want to be in one or two years and start planning now, while you are reading these words.

In my own life, I have had to make such changes several times. For quite a few years I have been traveling to speak to various Christian groups. Previous to this, I had several different jobs outside of ministry, but the most difficult change I have had to make was within the ministry.

For several years I traveled nationwide to smaller churches to teach congregations and advise pastors. During that time I was not doing a very good job of supporting my wife and three children. Little churches do their best to help traveling ministers, but weekly love offerings of $50 to $300 just did not feed my family very well. I wanted to change my circumstances, but I had the added pressure of feeling that I should be trusting God. Subconsciously, I felt that sooner or later God would look down from heaven, maybe feel sorry for me or at least want to reward me for my service, and then supernaturally provide an abundance. It did not work that way. We struggled year after year, often with very little food in our house. Then I watched as our car was being repossessed because we could not make the payments.

God did reach down from heaven to answer my cry, but the answer came in the form of a revelation—a light went on as an inner voice said, "Harold, you are going to have to do something different!" I decided to change things. I believe it was the Lord giving me the strength to change, but the help I needed was not a big amount of money, as I previously thought, rather it was a kick in the pants. (Thank you, Lord.) The revelation that came to me was that if I wanted to have more money, then I would have to get more money. *Eureka!*

Ministering in all those little churches was not providing enough money for my family, so I was going to have to think of some way to change that. Understand, I not only had to break out of my comfort zone, but also I had to challenge strong chains of "spiritual thinking." I had felt good, right, and even holy about unselfishly giving my time to those small churches. I also felt obligated to them. However, I needed to face reality. To continue ministering to God's people, I needed money. I needed a plan that would bring in more finances. First, I decided to preach from time to time at bigger churches which could help us more financially. Now, that is not just a simple step. It meant building relationships with pastors of larger churches. It meant planning my schedule at least six months ahead, since big churches schedule speakers that far in advance, whereas smaller ones only think two weeks in advance. Also, I had to be a little more professional and presentable—I had to believe in myself and alter my lifestyle.

Sometime Christians have a difficult time picturing ministers consciously making such decisions. They would rather have ministers floating around waiting on God mysteriously to guide their way. Phooey! That's ridiculous! I am trusting God by stepping out to do what I have to do to provide for my family (and so should you). That is true faith!

Second, I decided to market my books. I previously had been "depending on God" to cause people to order my books through the mail. Well, that is not trusting God. That attitude is permeated with laziness and blindness. Proverbs says,

A little sleep, a little slumber,
A little folding of the hands to rest,

Then your poverty will come as a robber,
And your want like an armed man.

(Prov. 24:33-34)

I decided I should trust God by getting off my backside and coming up with a plan to get thousands of my books into the hands of people. I would do what I had to do to create a constant flow of my books into the hands of the Body of Christ. That would take time, money, and planning. So that is what I am doing.

Third, I decided to raise supporters, that is, Christian people who love and believe in my ministry, to financially support us on a monthly basis. That is easier said than done. Again, I would have to change. I had to overcome my fear of talking about money. I had to regard money not as a dirty, embarrassing subject, but as a commodity, precious and holy to God, something which I needed in order to do God's work. I had to overcome my related guilt and fears.

These changes were not easy. Change never is. But unless you change, next year at this time you will be in the same position financially as you are right now.

Did you hear that?

Take out a piece of paper and write down all the things you wish you could do in life related to work. Don't just do this in your head. I said take out a piece of paper and write these things down. You're thinking, "Who is he to talk to me this way?" Well, for right now, consider me your mother, so hurry up and get that paper out!

Now take a pen—and brainstorm. It is good to be a dreamer right now. In a moment we will look at the list realistically, but now you should have the freedom to write down every desire which you wish you could fulfill. No one else is going to see your sheet, so go ahead and write down anything and everything related to jobs you always have wanted to do during your life. Dream the impossible. Throw off the chains and restrictions for a moment. Do not discount yourself by concluding that something will be impossible.

I am pausing now, waiting for you to fill up a piece of paper.

Done? OK, let's examine your dream list more realistically. You are not going to be an astronaut nor inherit a billion dollars, so cross those off. Putting those down was good because I wanted you to think freely, but now we are looking through a realist's eyes.

Look at your list again. There are certain job interests which you may have that simply never will produce prosperity. The fact is that poverty-minded people tend to choose jobs which produce poverty. Prosperous people gravitate toward careers which produce abundance.

Earlier we mentioned that a physician makes more money than a carpenter. This is a fact. I do not mean to put the carpentry career in a negative light. The truth is that I personally love carpentry work but I have had to face personal decisions about this myself. Comparing a carpenter with a doctor is like comparing two people in a race, one riding a tricycle and the other a motorcycle. If you are going to try to cross the country in one or the other, I recommend the motorcycle.

This may seem simplistic, but you need to think this clearly about your job selection. You never will become financially successful working at a job that pays minimum wage. Face this reality. The reason many people cannot get ahead financially is not because God hates them, nor because the devil is after them, but because they have a low-paying job.

Poverty-minded people sometime deceive themselves about these issues. For example, if a poverty-minded person is considering a job as a carpenter, he may justify his own desires by thinking of the one week each year when he can do a job that brings in a big payoff (the short stretch along the road where his tricycle will roll fast downhill), rather than the other 51 weeks during which he struggles. A poverty-minded salesman will set his thoughts on the established salesman who made a big sale that brought him instant wealth. In contrast, the prosperous-minded person considering a job in sales is able to look realistically at all salesmen and see how each is doing over the course of many years.

If you want a realistic view, a prosperous view, look at other people who are doing the type of work you are considering. Do not listen to the occasional success stories. Look at everyday reality.

If you want to prosper, you must deal with the truth. Lies put you into bondage, truth sets you free—even from poverty.

Poverty-minded people often choose low-income employment, but then continue living in dreamland. They realize they have a low-paying job but they continue hoping for some amazing breakthrough. They will not face the fact that so much income only goes so far. They live like gold-seekers, digging and working hard in hopes that they will find the big nugget. It is the lottery mentality carried over into their career choice.

Reality dictates that if a person wants to prosper, they must do something that produces prosperity.

Before you choose a new career, examine the financial state of others in that career. If you want to be a secretary, look at other people doing the type of secretarial work you hope to do. What kind of car are they driving? What type of home do they have? If you want to be a computer programmer, notice how financially successful other programmers are. If you want to work in a hospital, talk to people already doing the work you want to do.

Next, consider the location where you will have to live in order to make a good living. A secretary working in New York City will make much more than a secretary working in a small rural farming community. Face reality about where you will have to locate to make a better living.

If other people typically remain poor doing the type of work you want in the region you want, then guess what? You are not going to get rich doing what they are doing.

Do not have a lottery mentality about this. Do not allow yourself to think, "Well, I am different!"

You are not different! You are a human being with 24 hours a day. If most of the other people in that business are not getting rich, then you won't either.

Now, I am not telling you what job to choose, nor to choose employment solely based on financial rewards. I simply am asking you to face reality. Again, let me say that if you are happy working at a job that pays your bills but does not allow you to become rich, that is OK. If you love your present work, then keep doing it. If you want to change careers and go into work that does not produce much income, that is OK. But do not deceive yourself into thinking that someday you will be rich.

Face this reality. People are not paid by how hard they work, as much as they are paid by what type of work they are doing. It is not how fast you pedal your tricycle, but your willingness to get off your tricycle and onto a motorcycle, or into a car, or better yet, into an airplane.

Check your list. With a realistic mind, cross off careers that will not produce for you the lifestyle you desire.

What is left over? Ask yourself, "Which of these remaining careers can I possibly get into if I set a goal to be there four years from today?" Please do not let that length of time scare you. Rome was not built in a day. It is time to be realistic. How long is required for you to make changes may be determined by your circumstances. Some parents have to face the reality that they will be unable to change careers until their children graduate. Some divorced people with whom I have worked must realize they are obligated to court-ordered financial arrangements. Other people have commitments to their company.

Be realistic. Changing careers may take time, but you need a goal now. If you really want to change jobs, you can. If you want to be in a completely different field of work, one that pays better money, one that is more rewarding, you can do it.

I remember when my father made his big break. He worked as a barber most of his life. Things were difficult for my parents, especially when all six young children were at home. When I was in grade school my father did his best, but his barbershop was located in a very depressed area of town where very little business came to his door. I have no idea how long he dreamed and planned, but one day he broke out of that environment. He decided. Dad rented a space for his barbershop in the brand new mall in town. Then on a simple copy machine he made hundreds of fliers advertising that new barbershop. Suddenly, our family was swept into motion. We passed out those fliers door to door throughout the surrounding neighborhoods. As a young boy, I can remember how exciting it was. Things were changing and I knew it. And they did. God blessed us.

I admired my father for making that bold step in his life. It takes courage to change. There is always a risk. Often it is uncomfortable.

You may need training for your next career. Perhaps you think you are too old—that is your poverty mind-set putting you into prison. Many people mistakenly think that only younger people can learn and handle the pressures of a university or community college. That is a lie. The truth is that mature adults today do much better in school in many ways than young adults do, and they are flooding back into the schools of higher learning at an amazing rate.

You say you do not have time. Another lie. Take a night class. Learn how to operate a computer. Learn a foreign language. Learn how to manage a business. Learn accounting. Learn something!

You may have to take a year or more of schooling. So what? Why should all those young college boys get the high-paying jobs? It might as well be you taking home that fat paycheck. You may have to sell your house and use the equity to rent a cheaper place while you go to school. Do not be scared away by the price of higher education. Many students make it through by holding down a part-time job while going to school. It is not that hard.

What you need is a goal, a plan. It may take you some time to think it all out, but that is OK. Start dreaming. Think about it this week. Start formulating in your mind how you could do it. Take the next month or so and just start dreaming.

What we are trying to get you to do is escape the complaining, feeling bad, grumbling, I-can't-do-anything mode, and get you into the someday-I-will-do-greater-things mode. Shift gears.

After you have some ideas, go investigate. Look on your calendar for your next day off. Decide to go and talk to someone. Telephone the technical trade school in town or visit the employment office. I know it is tough to walk through those doors, and you may be embarrassed if someone you know sees you there, but six years from today it will be you driving the new car when they will see you again. When you go into the employment service, you do not have to look at the available jobs. You might be better helped by simply talking to one of the personnel workers there about available programs to help you get more schooling, training, financial help, or whatever. Just relax and talk. Let them give you ideas.

Talk to people who are in the work in which you would love to be. Read materials about it. Keep your ears open.

Do not be under pressure to make decisions. Right now all you are doing is formulating a dream. It is a year or several years from now for which you are planning.

This is important. Change begins with a person thinking about change. If you do not dream today, nothing is going to change, and you will be in exactly the same position financially at this time next year. Nothing will change unless you start thinking. But thinking, in time, produces results. What you think today, you can be tomorrow.

Finally, let me say that some people seem to be waiting around for someone else to give them permission to dream, plan, and go on with their lives. Well, I give you permission. Better yet, give yourself permission. Best of all, you do not need permission. Start. It is OK.

Worksheet to Help You
Consider a Career Change

1. Dream. List below all the work-related things you would enjoy doing someday. Brainstorm. Put everything down.

_____

_____

_____

_____

_____

_____

_____

_____

_____

_____

_____

_____

(Before step two, you may want to dream for a few days about other things you can add to the above list.)

2. Now be realistic. Cross off the above list the myths and ridiculous.

3. Think of people you know who are in the types of employment you have listed. If those people are struggling financially, face reality and cross out those types of employment.

35

4. For the remaining ideas on your list, write down steps you could take during the coming year to secure more information, receive more training, talk to people, etc.

_____

_____

_____

_____

_____

_____

_____

_____

_____

_____

I have had the privilege not only of knowing some wealthy people, but also of contrasting on a large scale how wealthy and poverty-minded people think. In my travels to many foreign countries, I have been able to observe how people think in third-world countries compared with how they think in industrious, prosperous areas of the world. This has made clear some glaring distinctions.

For example, in remote regions of the Philippines, I have been amazed at how terrible traveling conditions are. Several times I have made long bus trips across rough roads. We have broken down more than once en route. Each time the driver would get out to fix the problem with whatever tools he had brought along. It was obvious he was jerry-rigging the bus just to get us back on the road. Other vehicles along the primitive roads were loaded beyond their maximum capacity, often with boxes, animals, and sometime people riding on the roofs. Everyone seemed interested only in reaching their immediate destination, with no thought of taking care of their vehicles and keeping things running long-range.

Similar thought patterns keep those roads in terrible conditions, with huge potholes, jutting rocks, and washed-out areas. On one trip I noticed heavy equipment alongside the road. I had hopes that something would be done to improve the conditions of the road we traveled, but day after day, the big road grader just sat there not being used. When I asked about it, I was told it was very difficult to get anyone who lived in the area to operate the equipment. Because their minds were focused only on short-term needs, they would not stay on the job for any length of time. If a man was hired in the morning, he very often would walk off the job as soon as he had made enough money to pay for the needs of himself and his family for that day. He saw no need to keep working, because his immediate needs were met. Even more discouraging is that this short-term mind-set keeps people from ever learning how to operate such equipment.

(Do not form the wrong image of the Philippines. The developed areas are much more modern and the people think more long-term, as do those in prosperous countries.)

Prosperous people think and act with long-range goals in mind. Today's labor may not pay off until years later. And that is OK for the prosperous-minded person. He looks at his life as though he was high above, viewing the whole span of his time on earth.

In contrast, poverty-minded people live and act only for today.

These differences are obvious when we talk about major thought patterns in different regions of the world, but they are also evident in our lives. The first difference is in the use of credit cards. Poverty-minded people quickly will grab a credit card, if they have one, in order to fulfill their present need or desire. The moment they are making the transaction with that card, they block out of their mind the future consequences. They think in terms of today, not tomorrow.

Prosperous people may use credit cards, but they never lose sight of the future.

People just learning to break out of poverty should destroy their credit cards. They are not capable of handling them. It is like giving a child a gun. Until they grow up, they will be unable to know how far that bullet can travel and how dangerous it is. Credit cards are guns that shoot bullets into your future. They will blow holes in it, killing your chances at future prosperity.

People need to mature before ever being entrusted with a credit card. They need to think bigger if they want to prosper. They need to look at their life from higher above. If they can see life from a higher plane, they will realize that they are robbing and destroying their future every time they borrow money through the use of credit. You cannot expect a good future if you are robbing from that future. This is obvious if you have developed a prosperous perspective of your own life.

Prosperous people are able to make investments today which will pay off years down the road. The need for this or the ability to accomplish this escapes the poverty-minded person. When told to save or invest, objections leap in his mind, "I have needs today!" "How can I save when I am barely paying my present bills?" It is difficult for that person to hear the very words that will help in his present situation. He is so locked into small thinking, that he never will get out. Yes, he must pay his present bills, but today's decisions should be based on a long-range view of his life.

Rise higher. That is the answer.

Poverty-minded people have a difficult time setting goals or verbalizing their plans for the future. When my wife and I first were married we attended a small meeting where everyone was asked to write down their financial goals. People around us then read some of their goals, such as buying a home, paying for their children's education, going on a vacation, etc. When it was time for my wife and me to speak, we had nothing to say, and to tell you the truth, I actually was proud of it. I can remember thinking how selfish and money-seeking all those other people seemed to be. I had goals about serving God, accomplishing certain things in ministry, and raising a Christian family, but not goals related to money. I left that meeting feeling more holy than the rest.

I was a fool, and a poor one at that.

This became more obvious years later when I was invited to the home of a wealthy friend to meet for two days with about ten other men, all of whom were prosperous. I was the pauper in the bunch.

When the meeting started, we first introduced ourselves by going around the room and telling a little about what we do and who we are. One person after another shared about his career, his future, and his heritage. That last part was a surprise to me. Each shared how his father, grandfather, and/or great-grandfather accomplished certain tasks. They mentioned the country from which their ancestors came, while everyone listened with great interest.

At my turn I had little to say. I mentioned my present ministry, but I had nothing to tell about my past. My grandfathers had died before I was born, and I knew almost nothing about my heritage. Besides, I thought, who cares? I rationalized that I am a Christian with God as my Father.

Looking back, I realize those prosperous men had a long-range view of life. They even thought "generationally." They were aware of their family lineage and the people from whom they had descended. It was a part of their identity.

In recent years, I have learned the importance of thinking generationally. I have learned it not only leads to prosperity, but it's the biblical way of thinking—God's way of thinking. It used to trouble me that the Bible recorded so many genealogies. Who cares who descended from whom? I could not see the significance because in my poverty mindset, I could not relate.

But it is a key to prosperity!

Think of the rich young boy raised in a mansion by his parents who have everything financially they ever wanted. This boy's name is John Richard III. Many poverty-minded people coming in contact with John Richard III might chuckle within, thinking John Richard III is a spoiled brat. There was a time when I sarcastically would have thought, "I wonder what little Johnny is doing for fun these days." My attitude toward Johnny would be condescending because I did not understand the family's lifestyle, nor the significance of his name.

Consider John Richard III through prosperous eyes. Even his name declares who he is. That little boy is being groomed to think generationally. He will, therefore, be more able to handle great wealth successfully as an adult. In contrast, a poverty-minded person, even if given great wealth, would be more likely to lose it all. This is a fact!

You must think long-range. You must train yourself to set goals and view life from a higher plane.

Take a moment right now and think about your financial situation for your retirement years. Objections may rise within you such as, "Christians just need to trust God for their future!" "I am young and I have too many immediate needs!" "I will do it later!" If these are your thoughts, then I am confident in telling you that you have a poverty mindset. Your present financial position is below what it should be. Wisdom to handle your finances today is based on your ability to see tomorrow. If you cannot see tomorrow, you are blind today.

Go on being blind if you want to, or have the sense to declare, "Once I was blind, but now I see!"

One Christian teaching that hindered me from thinking long-range was that of the soon return of Jesus Christ. I had been taught for many years that we should expect Jesus to appear in the clouds at any moment. I'm not challenging that doctrine, but I want you to see how that doctrine sometime robs Christians of a long-range view of life. Had I known two decades ago that Jesus would not have come back yet, I would have planned better for the future (which is today's present). Again, I am not challenging any doctrine; rather I am trying to get you to see farther down life's road. Only if you are able to break through and see beyond your present limitations will you take on a more prosperous way of thinking.

One evening after I spoke in a church, an elderly Christian man came up to me and proudly said, "I want to die with nothing in my pocket because I want to constantly give away everything I have." Such a statement may sound "spiritual" and even honorable to some. However, what came out of his mouth next put things in perspective: "The problem is I have never had much money to give away." Unfortunately, this man could not see the connection between his lifetime of poverty and his way of thinking. I hope you will make the connection.

Think about your future. Take out a piece of paper and write down thoughts about what condition you want to be in during your retirement years. (If you have been under strong teaching concerning the soon return of Jesus, you may have to block that out of your mind for a moment just so you can punch through to see the future.) Write down what you would like to pass on to your children and even your grandchildren. Make yourself think about these things, even if it is hard. If possible, attend a meeting where people actually sit down under the guidance of a financial advisor and talk about future plans. The sooner you do these things, the sooner you will develop the thinking necessary to produce today's financial success.

Long-range thinking will help you succeed—not only tomorrow, but also today. The biggest reason is that a mind that is set on the long-term goal produces patience today. Poverty-minded people are impatient. They may try to be patient, but it is impossible. Their lives are oriented to the present. Time has been shrunk into small increments. For the prosperous person, time stretches out and, therefore, patience is a natural by-product. A heart of patience produces wealth, and it is impossible truly to be patient unless you have a long-range mind-set.

A long-range mind-set makes you act differently in everything you do today. When you buy a car, naturally you want it to run for as long as you own it. When you buy something at the store, you automatically consider whether or not it has a warranty or was made by someone who will stand behind his work. When you fix something, you want it to stay fixed. You are not like the Filipino bus driver jerry-rigging the bus just to get it to its next destination, but you take the extra time necessary to ensure it will not break down again. A long-range mind-set may slow your present rate of action, but it greatly increases your prosperity day by day.

Picture two men—rich Tom and poor George—each doing their own yard work. Tom is rich, George is poor. Tom does not have to tend his own yard, but he does since he enjoys it. George has many different wild grasses in the lawn and a few weed-ridden flower beds along his house. He does not give them much care because he figures he won't be living there long anyway. He just wants to finish the task so he can go on to his next immediately-pressing chore.

Tom planned his yard. Before it even was put in, he chose grass that grows well in his climate, holds up well under foot traffic, and does not need to be mowed very often. In the flower beds, he planted perennials with a surrounding plastic ground cover so he never has to pull weeds. It took Tom over two years to establish his lawn, but now it should not need any major work for years to come.

Each time poor George finishes yard work, he hurries into the house because his mind is set on another immediate job pressing on his mind. He even may leave out his garden tools, thinking he will have "more time later"—a recurring thought in the poverty mind. Tom, on the other hand, likes to finish things right. He is more likely to pick up his tools when finished because he wants his tools to last a lifetime, and he is not focused on the next immediate job.

A prosperous man once counseled me at a time I desperately needed it. I was anxious, with a thousand thoughts racing through my mind—most of them were ministry-related because I was pastoring a church at the time. I shared my immediate needs with that financially-successful church member. I wanted him to act, to help as soon as possible. Instead, he calmly looked at me and said, "I have learned that things have a way of working themselves out." He was prosperous. I was not.

Worksheet to Help You
Think Long-Range

1. Think about your foreparents.* Write down the names of your grandparents and great-grandparents going back as many generations as you can. Note their nationalities.

_____

_____

_____

_____

_____

_____

_____

_____

_____

_____

_____

_____

_____

_____

_____

*Some people have such a painful past that it is difficult for them to think about their foreparents; it is important to point out that all people have some good characteristics. If it is even too hurtful to consider those positive aspects, then a person can turn their attention simply to think historically without thoughts of relatives. This also will help develop a long-range view of life.

2. Envision your future and imagine the last five years you will be alive. List what you would like to be doing then. Think in terms of the categories mentioned below:

Your living environment:

_____

_____

_____

Your retirement income:

_____

Your hobbies and free-time activities:

_____

_____

_____

The inheritance you will leave:

_____

_____

_____

_____

_____

CHAPTER 5

Think In Terms Of Family Wealth

In Volume I, chapter 7, I told you about my embarrassment when I boasted to two wealthy men about making over $20 per hour picking wild mushrooms. The room fell silent and it dawned on me that they thought on a completely different level than I.

They thought in terms of "net worth." When they talked about wealth, it was not in terms of an hourly wage. In fact, they did not care what they themselves made each hour of each day. Instead, they were ever aware of the wealth they already had accumulated, including their home(s), automobiles, investments, businesses, etc. They were concerned primarily about managing their wealth so it would increase over the years.

I wanted to learn that way of thinking.

Before proceeding I must answer the questions which come to the mind of the sincere Christian: Does God want us to think in terms of net worth? Is this a godly perspective? Or should we live day to day, hour by hour, trusting Him? What is God's will for our lives? Which is right?

To answer these, let me state point-blank: hand-to-mouth living is not God's will. I want to convince you of this because it will change your life and open your mind to a more prosperous way of thinking.

Consider the lifestyle God arranged for His people in the Old Testament times, after they came out of the wilderness and entered into the Promised Land. It was under God's explicit instructions that the land promised to the Israelites was divided into sections for each family. He called it their inheritance and instructed that each family would possess their portion for all the generations to follow. If any family lost its inheritance through bad financial dealings, mismanagement, or other problems, there were provisions whereby they would receive it back again. Every 50 years came the Year of Jubilee, at which time the land was to return to whatever family God originally had given it. The Jewish economic system was centered around the inheritance and family possessions. This was by God's design.

As I have been exposed to different cultures in the world around us, I have noticed that same thinking among today's prosperous peoples. The Jews, for example, still tend to think this way. Although they may not own land or center their lives on a place, they still seem to have as an anchor to their financial lives "the family wealth." They do not think of themselves as independent units but rather as a part of a family working together for success.

Many of the Orientals who migrate do so with a *family wealth mentality*. The parents have saved enough money to move, become established, and then help their children get started. The children grow up with an understanding that they must help the whole family succeed. They don't work just for themselves, but for their parents, their brothers and sisters, and the generations to follow them. When they get their first job, many of them are required by their parents to start giving all or a portion of their pay into the family wealth fund. That money must remain there until the parents decide when the children need it, which is usually at the time of their marriage, higher education, home purchase, or business start-up. The children actually get much more out of the account than they put in during their growing years, but it is managed by the parents.

Many cultures in the world have this mentality, such as wealthy Arab families in the Middle East, the upper class of India, the nobility of Europe, etc.

Poverty-minded people live as independent agents with no concept of the family's net worth. They live day to day for themselves. If they do have children, they see themselves providing for the young ones only while they are growing up. It is a temporary responsibility. When the children leave home, the parents return to their living-for-self lifestyle. They have no lasting concept of family wealth.

Unfortunately, many Christians have the poverty mind-set. They think it is spiritual and godly. They never have been taught any differently, nor have they been shown how God instilled in the Jewish people an inheritance consciousness which does, indeed, produce wealth for themselves and their descendants.

A prosperous farmer once quoted to me a Bible verse which was very important to his life:

> *The good man leaves an inheritance to his children's children.* (Prov. 13:22a)

When I was first shown this verse, I had a difficult time accepting its validity. I thought maybe it meant a spiritual inheritance or perhaps it was meant only for the Old Testament Jews. I reasoned that God had another way for Christians to live today that did not require planning or saving for the future. Besides, I was having a hard enough time just paying that week's bills, let alone thinking of my children's or grandchildren's financial position. Since then, I have become convinced that it is godly to be conscious of your family's wealth and concerned about how it may be passed from generation to generation.

For some readers this may be difficult to receive. You may have objections arising in your mind. Perhaps, like me, you never have considered seriously leaving an inheritance to your offspring. If you always have lived day to day, you probably have felt pretty good about it and even considered this simple lifestyle a godly way of life. Don't be defensive or feel condemned for living differently from what I am prescribing here. Please do not take my words that way. I am sorry if I am offending any readers; that is not my intention nor my heart. I have made these changes in my own life, and I simply am explaining to you that what I have discovered actually works. I am writing to help, not hurt.

An *inheritance consciousness* helps you think and act prosperously today. Viewing your financial situation from the net-worth perspective, rather than the hourly wage, is essential. It is a higher perspective. It is another way of looking down from above over the course of your life. It does work.

Consider then your net worth. Include all that you own, then subtract your bills, unpaid mortgage, and other liabilities. Notice that this is the first thing a banker will ask you to do if you apply for a loan. He looks at you from the net-worth perspective. All that you own, minus what you owe, is what you are worth financially.

Do not feel badly if you own very little or even if you are deep in debt. That is the whole point. You need to learn how to think. The issue is not how much you own; it is how you think. Think from above and look over whatever you own.

Now take dominion over it. See what you own and take responsibility in your heart for it. Tell God that you will act responsibly with what you presently have. Jesus said, *"For whoever has, to him shall more be given"* (Mark 4:25a). Until you "have" something, that is, take dominion over it and claim personal responsibility for it, the authority of God for that amount cannot flow through you. See it. Take it. Accept responsibility for it.

Now you are the manager of it. As a manager you now can begin to watch over it and help it increase year by year. This, and not your hourly wage, is your main concern. Once you see all that you own from above, you will find the energy and wisdom to do good things with it. You subconsciously will start to take better care of what you own. You will be more prone to keep oil in the car and paint on the house. You will be motivated to keep your house cleaner, and the children may even learn to keep their bicycles out of the rain. You also will take actions today that pay off in the future, something about which we will learn more in the next chapter.

Calculate Your Net Worth

Assets: Present Value:
Automobile #1   _____
Automobile #2   _____
Home   _____
Furniture   _____
Clothing   _____
Recreational equip.   _____
Savings   _____
Amt. in Checking   _____
Investments   _____
Misc. Possessions   _____
Total   _____

Liabilities:
Auto Loan #1   _____
Auto Loan #2   _____
Home mortgage   _____
Credit card #1   _____
Credit card #2   _____
Credit card #3   _____
Credit card #4   _____
Unpaid taxes   _____
Bills due   _____
Other liabilities   _____
Total   _____

Net worth:
Subtract total liabilities from
                    total assets: _____

Plant a seed and several months later that seed will produce dozens of seeds. Would you rather have the single seed or the handful of seeds produced from the one? Obviously, the handful is better.

The same thinking works with wealth. Investing is a way to plant financial seeds. If you invest a little seed today, it will grow into a harvest for tomorrow. If you learn how to invest on a regular basis, you soon will be living on the harvest instead of the initial seeds.

Jesus talked about investing in the parable of three men who received talents (Matt. 25:14-30). He explained that a certain man gave three servants a portion of his wealth to manage in his absence. One servant was given five talents, the second received two, and the third received one. (A talent was worth about $1,000 in silver, much more in buying power.) Our Lord taught in this parable how each servant managed differently the talents he was given. The first used his five talents to earn five more. The second made two more with his. These two profitable servants were praised by their master, who said to them,

> *"Well done, good and faithful slave;*
> *you were faithful with a few things, I*
> *will put you in charge of many things,*
> *enter into the joy of your master."*
> (Matt. 25:21)

In contrast, the third servant did not use the talent he was given, but rather hid it in the ground because he was afraid. When the master found out, he rebuked the servant, saying,

> *"You wicked, lazy slave ... you ought to*
> *have put my money in the bank, and*
> *on my arrival I would have received*
> *my money back with interest."*
> (Matt. 25:26-27)

Notice in this parable how Jesus spoke positively about the men who used their finances to invest and increase. The third servant, though, was called "wicked and lazy."

Sometime Christians today misinterpret this parable, because in the English language the word *talent* means, a *natural skill* or *ability*. Therefore, it is easy to misinterpret Jesus' words and reason that He was talking only about using our natural abilities for Him. Of course, that is important, but a talent in Jesus' days referred to a set amount of money; so He actually was teaching about how people use their finances to increase.

Think again of our Lord's words. The person who did not invest was called *wicked and lazy*. The two who invested wisely were commended: *"Well done...I will put you in charge of many things...."*

These principles are very basic for people who already are aware of how investments work; however, they are revolutionary for people coming out of a poverty mind-set. I know, because my mind has had to go through this paradigm shift. And that is what it is—a major shift in thought patterns.

Think like a cattle rancher. If a certain rancher starts with 10 cows and each year his herd doubles in size, then after one year he will have 20 cows, the second year 40, and the third year 80. Of course, those cows either will have to have twin calves or be giving birth to females. Plus, he may have to sell some cows to pay his taxes and other bills. If, however, that rancher can let the herd grow to a substantial size, he can become financially secure and blessed. After only seven years of doubling each year, those original 10 cows would multiply to the total of 1,280 cows. That's right, work it out for yourself on a piece of paper.

Year	# cows
0	10
1	20
2	40
3	80
4	160
5	320
6	640
7	1,280

A rancher with 1,280 cows (seven years) could relax and manage them wisely with much less work. Perhaps he would take each year's calves and sell them at the market. He could use the money, provide for his family, and even hire a ranchhand to care for the cattle the rest of his days.

All this may seem simplistic, and indeed it is. There is a lot of work to raising cattle, and I do not want to make it sound so easy. My aim, though, is to help you think like a rancher (or a farmer). If you can view your present wealth the way the rancher sees his cattle, you have taken a major step toward prosperity.

The key, now, is to start "managing your cattle" (or planting your seeds). Allow them to reproduce. Please make yourself think this way. It is easy to see what the rancher should do. Anyone of us could tell him to increase the size of his herd until it provides for him and his family—then life would be easy. Well, your possessions can take care of you, if you just think like a rancher.

There are many ways to do this. Perhaps you will be disappointed that this book is not meant to take that specific step for you, nor teach you how to invest. Rather, this book is written to teach you how to think and restructure your thought patterns. If you are ready for that next step, you need to learn from other writers about investments. You can buy a book at a local bookstore and just start learning. It's not hard. You can take a class at your local community college. It is easy to learn if you just do it gradually and do not put yourself under undue pressure. Better yet, just talk to an investment counselor and let him or her explain the basics to you. The appointment should be free for you and someday you may even decide to have that investment counselor do the work for you.

The key today is for you to become a manager of your possessions and start planting some seed. Allow me to just whet your appetite concerning the power of seed-planting. People who invest money know it is common to at least double their investment every seven years (this is true at the time of this writing by using mutual funds and other stock-related investments). These investments are neither high risk nor difficult. It is simply how money given to an average financial manager in America will reproduce itself with no work on your part.

Doubling every seven years may not sound like much if you are thinking of only a short time or a small amount. Consider, however, the value of a nice car today, perhaps $20,000. If that money was invested in the average mutual fund when a person was 21 years old, by the time he was 63 years of age, he would have $1,280,000. That is right—a million dollars would cost him only the price of a car at age 21—no work, just entrusting it to an investor. How would you like to have a million at your retirement?

Age	Amount
21	$20,000
28	$40,000
35	$80,000
42	$160,000
49	$320,000
56	$640,000
63	$1,280,000

There are costs along the way, and the government will try to take a large share of your profits through taxation if the investment is not handled correctly. Such matters are understood by the investment counselor or accountant who will do the work for you, if you just will give them the privilege of handling your money.

You may wonder if it is worth sacrificing. Should you buy a new car or put that $20,000 into an investment plan? Do you really want to give your children a million dollars when you die? Well, what if it was your grandfather trying to make this decision 42 years ago? Today you would have a million dollars. At a modest interest rate of 7%, you would be making more than $200 per day just by letting that money sit in an average investment account. Don't you wish your grandfather would have decided to invest? Instead of being Johnny today, you would be John Richard the Third!

If you were to set aside $20,000 and teach your descendants how to manage their wealth, rather than think by an hourly wage, all your descendants—from now on—could be millionaires.

Is it any wonder why some cultures seem to advance ahead of all the people around them? They think in terms of managing wealth.

You may never be able to hand $20,000 to an investor. That is OK. We are not really trying to get you to, unless, of course, you happen to receive a large amount of money at some point, such as an inheritance. Why not invest it instead of spending it on your immediate desires? If, however, you do not foresee a large amount ever landing in your hands, how about setting aside just a few dollars each month? A seed! Even $25 per month can produce a tremendous harvest down the road.

Poverty-minded people may regress to the lottery mentality at this point. They have heard stories of someone investing a hundred dollars in just the right market that has grown at a phenomenal rate. The poverty-minded person then thinks investing is a matter of finding that one rare chance deal. That is foolish. We are talking about *average* stock-related investments today. They double about every seven years. We are not talking about chance deals. We are talking about faithfully and diligently starting to set aside a little bit each month and letting that seed grow in the soil.

I want to teach my children how to prosper.

My oldest son, Joshua, was fifteen when he started working at a fast-food restaurant, his first regular job. It was a great place for him to work and to learn hard-work ethics. He wants to prosper. He is the kind of young man who wanted to buy stock in the company when he first began working for them. Because this is his nature, it was easy to teach him how to become prosperous—or maybe he is teaching me, I am not sure.

I once read a book on how to train your children to be prosperous. I decided to teach my own son some of the principles. Since the day Joshua got his first paycheck, he started to manage his finances. He would deposit every paycheck into his own bank account. Then he would write a check in the amount of 10% to give to God. About 10% more was used for investing. That left 80% which he could spend on his personal needs and desires. This developed in him good habits and it gave him great freedom with the 80% he had left. I do not want him investing all of his money because enjoying the fruit of one's labor is a good, healthy thing to do. However, I wanted him to develop a lifestyle of investing seed along the way.

How about you? Think like a farmer and learn how to plant some seeds.

I wish all Christians would grasp this concept. Unfortunately, many are sitting around waiting for God to perform a miracle. Some even are fixing their faith on such Bible verses as Proverbs 13:22b, *"And the wealth of the sinner is stored up for the righteous."* If those Christians simply applied the principles God has revealed in His Word, the wealth of the sinners would start flowing into their hands. Instead, they are waiting for God to fulfill His Word, while God is waiting for them to apply His principles.

Christians must recapture the financial arena. It is not just one or two, or an occasional Christian who should prosper. God wants to bless all His people. As a whole, we need to rise to the top. Jesus explained that the kingdom of God grows like a mustard seed (Matt. 13:31-32) and like leaven in a lump of dough (Matt. 13:33). The kingdom and authority of God will not manifest instantaneously by God's sovereign intervention. Our Lord compared its growth and manifestation in the earth with growing seeds. This is true for finances just as in every other area of life. Those who want authority in the financial realm must plant seeds today. This is how God works.

Do you see how powerful this is? Most people spend all their hard-earned money on immediate needs, week after week, month after month. Tomorrow's income is then based on what they can earn tomorrow. Farmers don't live that way. Tomorrow's income is based on what is planted today, and even a small amount planted today will yield a huge crop tomorrow.

How are you living? Will you be paying your bills this week with money that you earned this week? Or will you pay them with money earned one or two years ago? If you are living by the seedtime and harvest principle, you will be living on the harvest rather than the seeds. You can go on living by what you earn every day of your life, or you gradually can make the shift to managing your wealth and living off the harvest. Two different lifestyles are produced; in the second lies abundance.

While the farmer sleeps, his crop is growing. Likewise, financial seeds that you plant today will grow even while you are resting. This is what we call *making your money work for you, instead of you working for your money.* It is a wonderful, healthy feeling to have your money producing even while you are resting. You work hard during the seed-planting season of life, but it starts growing and reproducing itself in time.

This is not only wonderful, it is the pattern God placed in nature itself. People who grasp this simply are working with the natural pattern of life: seedtime and harvest. "Look at the lilies of the field; look at the birds of the air!" Learn from them. Don't be stupid. This is how life is supposed to work.

Earlier we compared the poverty mind-set of earning money with a person riding a tricycle. In order to get more money, they think they have to pedal their tricycle faster. You can advance by pedaling faster. You even can get ahead by changing your mode of transportation (meaning your type of employment), because there are some careers that will advance you quicker; however, sooner or later you need to get on an airplane and let someone else take you where you want to go. At first an airplane moves slowly, but once it is in the air it will take you to your destination much faster. Everyone has to walk or take a car or bus to the airport, but sooner or later you will want to buy a ticket to fly.

Allow me to suggest a wise plan. Start managing your income: give 10% to God and invest 10%. In the next chapter, we will talk more about the amount you give to God (and what you give in taxes to the government). Here, we want you to think in terms of planting seeds today.

Look everywhere for opportunities to plant seeds. For example, if you have a home mortgage, you can plant a seed every month simply by adding $25 to each payment. Make sure that $25 is applied to your principal. An extra $25 paid one time at the beginning of a 30-year mortgage will cut as much as $500 off the total amount you pay. Add $25 to each month's payment and you can save thousands.

You can pay seed amounts on other loans, such as those on your car or credit cards. The higher the interest rate on each item, the more you will save. Think of it as seed because it will produce tremendous rewards down the road.

Notice that these are investment plans already set up for you. You do not need to talk to an investment counselor. If you have a mortgage or other loans out, you already have perfect places to plant. However, it is also true that if you talk to a financial advisor your seed probably will yield a greater harvest in the future. Remember it is free to talk to most investment counselors. They want your business, and they will be happy to set up an investment plan for you. Do not talk to some unknown financial guy who works out of a shabby office. Instead, go to a reputable business. Don't buy into anything right away, but start talking to someone about how to set up an investment plan.

If you simply do not have cash to plant, you still need to think in terms of seed planting and harvest. For example, a wise salesman is not out merely to make the deal today. Instead, he is continually planting seeds in the hearts and minds of future customers and, hence, cultivating a farm.

If you have dreamed about starting a new job someday, invest one hour every evening in that future career. Look for a business opportunity that will require just a *seed amount of time* now, but pay off big ten years from today. I like writing books, even though what I write now usually will not be published and read by others until months or even years later. You will be a wise farmer by investing time reading books today that will make you a better person tomorrow. If there is someone who could help you years later in your career, phone them and start a *seed relationship* today. Take an afternoon to look around your home and make it more energy efficient; one hour invested in plugging drafty holes may save you hundreds of dollars in your heating and cooling bills over the course of the next ten years. When you build things around your home, take the extra time to make sure they will last for years and years. Invest time, friendship, a smile, yourself, etc. Start farming.

Think this way with the people around you. If you are a boss, invest in your employees so they become, in time, your greatest investment. If you are a mother, plant encouragement in your children when they come home from school: they will be your harvest. If you are a minister, disciple individuals who eventually will accomplish great things in this world. For example, if a pastor spends five years discipling a young man who later becomes a youth minister, that pastor then will have an effective youth ministry with many young people under his care. Plant seeds in people.

Work for the future harvest. Stop looking for the immediate payoff. Move out of *today's earning mentality* (tricycle pedaling) and embrace a *farming mind-set* (airplane riding). Develop this as a lifestyle, and soon the harvest will overtake you. These are the facts of life.

Worksheet to Help You
Think Like a Farmer

1. Think of areas where you can plant seeds. Brainstorm. Locate the best soil.

On credit card debts: _____

On your car payments: _____

Toward your mortgage: _____

In an investment plan: _____

In a future business which you desire:

_____

_____

In seed relationships:

_____

_____

In your employees:

_____

_____

In your disciples:

_____

_____

In yourself through reading books, taking a class, learning the computer, etc.

_____

_____

_____

2. Seriously consider managing your income by giving 10% to God and investing 10% through a professional financial advisor. Calculate those amounts below:

    a. Determine your total monthly income.

Salary	_____
Commissions	_____
Benefits	_____
Investment Income	_____
Interest Income	_____
Other Income	_____

                         Total   _____

    b. Calculate the following percentages.

    10% of the total to give to God
        (multiple the above total by .10) _____
    10% of the total to invest
        (same as last amount calculated) _____

3. Start farming by planting those seeds. Do it diligently and faithfully. Never eat your seeds until they become full heads at harvest time.

Some Christians, no matter how hard they work, budget, and plan, seem to remain financially cursed. Is it possible that they really are living under a curse? Yes. Financial curses are identified clearly in the Bible. Spiritual forces do, indeed, hold back some people. We will mention the two most common curses and explain how to break free.

The first curse relates to the negative forces released upon those who neglect or refuse to pay taxes. The Apostle Paul wrote to the early Christians instructing them to submit to the governing authorities and pay taxes to them:

> *Let every person be in submission to the governing authorities. For there is no authority except from God, and those which exist are established by God. Therefore he who resists authority has opposed the ordinance of God; and they who have opposed will receive condemnation upon themselves...for it is a minister of God...Render to all what is due them; tax to whom tax is*

*due; custom to whom custom; honor to
whom honor.*   (Rom. 13:1-7)

Notice from these verses that every government
has God's backing. Of course, we acknowledge that
there may be individuals in positions of authority
who are making decisions contrary to the will of
God, however, government is still a "minister of
God." Because of this, we are told to honor them
and pay taxes. In addition, Christians are warned
that those who resist their government will receive
"condemnation," that is, a curse upon their own
lives.

Some people will justify their refusal to pay
taxes by arguing that they are not receiving anything in return for their money. They feel the
government is stealing their hard-earned cash. In
reality though, they still are living in that country,
driving on the roads, relying on their military defense, and conducting business under the established order. The fact is that no single person pays
enough to cover the costs of even the highway on
which they drive, nor the defense they receive, etc.
Every person (at least everyone who will read this
book), in every developed country on this earth,
receives more from their government than that for
which they pay. And that includes you!

Some people try to justify their neglect of paying taxes because of some evil they see within their
authorities. Such thinking is groundless. The above
instructions about submitting and paying taxes
were written by the Apostle Paul to the Christians

living in Rome, the very capital of the Roman government which at that time was persecuting Christians and engaging in many idolatrous activities. Paul told those Christians to pay taxes!

The issue of submission is bigger than what we receive back or whether or not we trust the government. It is in respect to God that we must submit. Paul explained that no government exists which has not been established by God. To resist authority, then, is to resist God. That is what the Apostle Paul was teaching the early Christians.

If you want God's blessings of prosperity, you willingly must pay taxes to the government. Notice the word, *willingly*. To *submit* means to *yield*. Stop fighting. This does not mean anyone should pay more than their share. On the contrary, people should manage their finances in such a way that they do not have to pay more than is required. However, they must pay that amount without grumbling (Phil. 2:14). Any time people resist or begrudge authority, they bring themselves under a curse. Only a change in attitude will free them from that curse.

I do not know how to state this any more clearly. I talk to people about their financial lives all the time, but sometime they simply will not hear this foundational truth. Some will get themselves involved in groups that jointly refuse to pay taxes. Others will sit around drinking coffee and complaining about the authorities of their nation. Such heart attitudes are foolish and self-destructive. I have repeatedly seen that people, including Christians, who get themselves involved in such activities are financially cursed.

There is nothing wrong with trying to change the government through established avenues of change; indeed, Christians should do everything they can to influence their country toward godly values. However, to resist that which is established is to resist God. Why would anyone do that? It's stupid. Don't do it and don't get involved with others who do.

An astounding truth is given to us in Malachi, chapter 1, which we will quote shortly. What we trust you will see is this: whoever or whatever has authority, deserves honor, and that which is honored has the right to receive from our financial increase first and foremost. Malachi writes as if this were the reasonable thing for the government to expect. It is reasonable that the government of any nation receives taxes, and that they take those taxes off the top of each person's income. Before a person pays their other bills, buys food, etc., they should pay taxes to their government. It is an issue of respect to authority.

This brings us to the second curse which we now can discuss and from which we can find freedom. The writer of Malachi compared our giving to the government with our giving to God. He pointed out that the government will not receive our "leftovers" after we pay our other bills. How much more important it is that people give to God, a greater and more deserving Lord:

> *"'A son honors his father, and a servant his master. Then if I am a father, where is My honor? And if I am a master, where is My respect?' says the Lord of hosts to you...."* (Mal. 1:6)

This exhortation was directed to the priests, but then God addresses all the Jews concerning their attitude toward Him as Master and Father. Under their economic system, they were expected to offer gifts from their crops and farm animals. In honor to God, they were expected to bring the first and the best:

> *"But when you present the blind for sacrifice, is it not evil? And when you present the lame and sick, is it not evil? Why not offer it to your governor? Would he receive you kindly?" says the Lord of hosts.* (Mal. 1:8)

The issue here is honor and respect. God expects to be treated better than the government. If He is Lord, then we must bow.

After explaining to the people that they must bring the first of their increase to Him, God explained the curse that would come upon them if they refused:

> *"If you do not listen, and if you do not take it to heart to give honor to My name," says the Lord of hosts, "then I*

*will send the curse upon you, and I
will curse your blessings; and indeed I
have cursed them already, because you
are not taking it to heart."* (Mal. 2:2)

By pointing out these Bible verses, I am telling
you to "get your act together." Prioritize! Give to
God what is God's and to Caesar what is Caesar's.
Use your money according to what you believe.

Firstfruits, that is, the first of all you earn,
belongs to the Lord. Proverbs teaches:

*Honor the Lord from your wealth,
And <u>from the first of all your produce</u>;
So your barns will be filled with plenty,
And your vats will overflow with new wine.*
(Prov. 3:10; emphasis added)

Notice the blessings that are promised to you in
return.

Malachi discussed further how to turn the
curse into a blessing. He sounded forth God's
words, saying,

*"You are cursed with a curse, for you
are robbing Me, the whole nation of
you! Bring the tithe into the storehouse, so that there may be food in My
house, and test Me now in this,"* says
the Lord of hosts, "if I will not open for
you the windows of heaven, and pour

out for you a blessing until it over-
flows. Then I will rebuke the devourer
for you...."   (Mal. 3:9-10)

God expected the people to tithe, which means to
bring the first ten percent of all they earn and give
it to Him.

Some Christians refuse to tithe because they
think it was meant only for the Jewish people in
the Old Testament. It is true that the Jewish
people made tithing a law, and we as Christians
are not under a law. However, here we are not
talking about a law. No. We are dealing with our
lives being in submission to the One we call Lord.
Is He Lord, or is He not? Does He deserve the
firstfruits of all we earn? Of course He does.

Turn your eyes away from the curses and look
at the promised blessings. God said He would *open*
the windows of heaven. Think about that. Earlier
we quoted Proverbs 3:10 where we are told that He
would *fill our barns with plenty* if we honored Him
with the firstfruits of our wealth.

Christians who do not believe in tithing have
not considered seriously these promises. If it is true
that the promises of tithing only work for Jews,
then we non-Jewish people got cheated. Imagine if
we could have the windows of heaven opened for us
simply by investing ten percent. If you really believed that God would open the windows of heaven
for you simply by your giving ten percent, then you
eagerly would apply this principle. When people
say tithing is not for them, what they really are
declaring is that they do not believe God will,

indeed, open the windows of heaven as He stated. They think tithing itself is a curse rather than the doorway to blessing. That is the real reason some people do not believe tithing is for them.

Please think about this. If I came to you and said, "Invest $100 and I will give you back $500," you either would jump at the chance or call me a liar. The only reason you wouldn't give me the $100 is because you didn't really believe I would give you back $500.

Now, I am not guaranteeing an immediate 500% return on what you give to God, but I am pointing out what is at the root of people's rejection of tithing. It is not because they think it was just for the Jews. No. It is because they do not believe God will keep His promise.

So then, how do we find out if tithing really works and if it is for us today? Try it! There is no other way. I can tell you how it has worked in my life and in the lives of others, but sooner or later you have to find out for yourself.

You can do this. God said, *"Test Me now in this, if I will not open for you the windows of heaven, and pour out for you a blessing until it overflows"* (Mal. 3:10). Nowhere else in the Bible are we told to test God. In fact, we clearly are forbidden to do so on any other point (Deut. 6:16).

What do you have to lose? If you were to test God on this for a few months, you would be risking some money and you even may be unable to pay your rent. So what? Listen, if this is really true, then it would be worth a few months' risk. If, indeed, God would keep His promise to open the windows of heaven, then you would enter into a whole new lifestyle—not only financially, but also in your relationship with God.

Several years ago when I pastored, I taught four straight weeks on the importance of tithing. Some people thought I was being pushy, but I had become totally convinced in my own life that God keeps His promises. So after teaching my congregation, I challenged them to test God. I asked them to write in their Bible the amount of their present income, including all benefits which they were receiving through employment, pensions or other means. Then I challenged them to tithe for four months, and at the end of that time we would make a comparison. Four months later I stood in front of the church and asked how many who had been tithing could say that they had received a *substantial raise* or *unexpected financial blessings* during our test period. Approximately 80% testified to the positive and some of the testimonies were amazing. (I wonder if the other 20% even tried tithing.)

Tithing works. What else can I say? People who think it is not for them are missing out on the greatest investment they possibly could make. Think of tithing like putting oil in your car. You would not run your car without oil in the engine, and in the same way you should not try to handle your finances without first giving to God. If you give the first of your income to God, the rest of your money will work better.

Here is the bottom line: Will God keep His promise?

What is God asking? The first ten percent of all you earn. As soon as you receive a paycheck, a commission, an investment dividend, or anything you can call income, set aside ten percent for God. Before you pay your bills. Before you go out for dinner. Before you pay the government taxes. Take ten percent of everything that comes into your hands and give it back to God.

How do you give a tithe to God? By freely giving it to whomever gives you spiritual food, strength, and blessings. The Apostle Paul wrote to those among whom he had discipled and labored, *"If we sowed spiritual things in you, is it too much if we should reap material things from you?"* (I Cor. 9:11) When God spoke through Malachi concerning the tithe, He said, *"Bring in the whole tithe into the storehouse, so that there may be food in my house"* (Mal. 3:10a). Where is the storehouse? Where spiritual food is. Ask yourself where you are being spiritually fed. Those are the places where you should give ten percent of your income.

You do not give that ten percent to your children, to your savings account, to your neighbor, to the poor, or even to the missionary in Africa. It is great to give to those needs, but that is not where the first ten percent goes. God will not rebuke the devourer on your behalf unless you follow His instructions. If you want God to open the windows of heaven you must give it to Him by bringing it into the storehouse where you are fed spiritually. That is how it works.

Again I say, "Test Him; try it."

Finally, in addressing thousands of Christians on various subjects, including prosperity, people sometime will ask me to pray for their financial situation. Occasionally, someone will ask me to "rebuke the poverty spirit" off of their life. I believe in prayer and in the power of blessing one another; however, I have a difficult time fulfilling this request because blessings come from God. One Old Testament prophet said, *"How can I curse whom God has not cursed?"* (Num. 23:8a). The answer to this is, of course, "I can't." No one effectively can curse or bless contrary to God's will.

I do not want to sound cold and harsh in this, but it is a fact that some people are blessed by God financially and others are not (Prov. 10:22). God *desires* to bless all of His children; however, God's blessings are conditional. If you want to be blessed, give the firstfruits to God and the second portion to your government. Do it with a willing heart.

It is not just tithing that opens the windows of heaven. It is a lifestyle of giving. To develop a prosperous soul, you must become more like God. God is a Giver.

This begins at home. If you want to be blessed by God, you need to bless your spouse and your children. I have seen that parents who do not desire to bless their children never enjoy prosperity. A prosperous soul is first of all manifested in one's own home.

Some Christians feel guilty about blessing their loved ones. They think all extra money should be used only to further the gospel, or their lives are structured around doing only what is most efficient and economical. Nonsense!

That is not the character of God. If that is how you perceive God, then that is how you will treat your loved ones. The truth is that God is not economy-structured the way tightwad human beings are. Just take a walk through nature some day and see all that God has made. Look at the beauty and magnificence of a tree or a mountain. A mountain is by no means an efficient use of dirt. God could have spread it out evenly to make more farmlands or thousands of other things more beneficial to man's productivity.

Even more revealing is to look again at the lily. This time hike back into the wilderness where perhaps no one else has been and stare at a flower. Probably no other human has looked at that flower, and yet God made it. And think that there are billions and billions of such flowers in the world that not one person ever will notice. That is the kind of God we have. Not everything He does is efficient in the sense of producing food, clothing, or shelter. In some ways, God is extravagant!

These issues are important! They must be settled in your mind before you buy your daughter her first car. Should you buy her a wreck, just enough to get her to school? Or is it right to spend a little more and buy her a newer vehicle? Do you have to justify in your mind spending that extra money, or can you do it just because you want to make her happy? Is it OK for you to be a giver?

I am trying to tell you that it is OK.

Answer these questions:

1. Husbands, can you buy your wife a present without having to rationalize that purchase?
2. Mothers, can you buy your son a nice coat without feeling guilty?
3. Is it OK to enjoy a nice dinner at the restaurant with your mate? Can you relax and enjoy life?

If you answered "yes" to these questions, then you know God's character. If you did not, then you have yet to discover the nature of God that we are revealing.

That's not to give license to wasting money or being careless. No. In Volume I, chapter 9, we discussed what is waste. Here we are trying to tell you that it is OK to use money to bless people— even if those blessings are nonessential.

The truth is that being a giver *is* good use of money.

If you cultivate giving as a lifestyle, God will reveal Himself more and more to you as a Giver. The Bible declares that to him who is perverted, God will reveal Himself as perverted; to him who is kind, God will reveal Himself as kind (II Sam. 22:26-27). It is that simple. To him who is a giver, God reveals Himself as a Giver.

Givers are blessed (Prov. 22:9). I have observed that people who bless others, wherever they go and with whomever they are, have more abundance. God somehow causes more blessings to flow their way. Tightwads and those who think only in terms of efficiency suffer and never experience God's best.

Do you want God to be abundant on your behalf? Then bless those around you, beginning in your own home.

It does not end there, however. It extends to the restaurant, when it is time to tip those who have served you. It goes to any employees you may have—take care of them and God will take care of you. Bless and you will be blessed.

Let's take this giving lifestyle one step further. In the Old Testament, God established for His people the Year of Jubilee. Once every 50 years everyone in the nation had to forgive all debts, at which time all property would return to the family that originally owned it. God established this as a law among the Jewish people.

Of course, we are not under the Old Testament laws, but the principle of giving is at the heart of God and good for people. It is a healthy thing to give things away from time to time. Clearing out your clothes closet and giving away anything you have not worn in several months is a healthy thing to do. It will unclutter your life and produce in you a more prosperous soul. Giving away that extra car may be just the step of faith you need to take in order to believe God for bigger and better things. Every once in awhile you need to go through the stuff you have accumulated and take a load to the local thrift store. Don't try to sell it. Just give it away. Your soul will be healthier.

When you give money, to whom should you give it? Of course, we are not talking here about the 10% you give to God. Rather, here we are talking about the extra money you use to help and bless people. Does it do any good to give five bucks to the guy standing on the corner? Should you help those poor starving children in Africa? Or should you help your cousin Barney who never has been able to keep a job?

Of course, you need to give as you feel God is leading you. Every Christian should be able to discern the leading of God in areas like this. However, it is helpful to consider general principles of giving. Handing $50 to the street alcoholic is not likely to help him in the long run. We need to use wisdom in how and to whom we give.

In this regard, I have learned much through my travels in third-world countries where people are sometime desperate. After giving to different individuals, I have observed how they handled the money and what resulted from their increase in wealth.

For example, I noticed that giving money to some people in the poorer areas of the Philippines leaves them in a worse condition than before. Because they are not able to deal with long-range goals, they will spend all of it immediately and become even more dependent upon outsiders to take care of them. It is a sad state of affairs to watch individuals and their extended families become helpless as "rich Americans" send them a monthly check.

On the other hand, I have seen wonderful results when helping people who already have goals and who are pursuing those goals with or without your help. We found an industrious Filipino pastor who was training natives to start their own churches. He was not waiting around for some American to give him money before he started his ministry. When we met him, he had about 15 students living in an area smaller than my garage. They had only a few books and not every student even owned a Bible. Yet that pastor already was overseeing more than a dozen churches in the remote regions and raising up more pastors to send out. So we helped him financially and found that we could boost his work greatly with only a small investment on our part.

That is the key. Find someone who is *doing* something good and help them succeed in it.

This is how God deals with us. He gives great amounts to the ones who will pursue their goals and go ahead no matter what. I have seen that people who wait around doing nothing because they have no money rarely will succeed or ever find the money they desire. On the contrary, people who use what they presently have to the best of their ability will find God's blessings working with them.

This issue is critical. God does not just give to people based on need. Of course, He feeds the sparrow and He is aware of every person on this earth. However, if He gave on the basis of need, then places like India would be receiving the greatest blessings today. Instead, God blesses people who apply His principles, have faith, and are advancing. Jesus taught this principle, saying,

> *"For to everyone who has shall more be given, and he shall have an abundance; but from the one who does not have, even what he does have shall be taken away"* (Matt. 25:29)

This is a hard concept for the poverty-minded person to embrace. They tend to think wealth should be distributed evenly among people. They are almost socialistic in their thinking and they perceive God as wanting to be socialistic, but somehow failing at it. In reality, God is not a socialist. He has no intentions of distributing wealth evenly. He takes care of all who will look to Him, but He blesses those who advance through accepting responsibility for their own lives.

Give like God gives and you will be blessed. Consider whom you should help as you are able. Do not waste your money. Give the hungry man standing on the street corner enough to buy one meal, but no more. Unless you clearly are led by God, don't give money to your cousin Barney who can't hold down a job. If he has children, offer to buy food for them, but don't reward Barney for his inactivity. It only will make him more of a dependent. *"If anyone will not work, neither let him eat"* (II Thess. 3:10b). That is how God gives. So also you should give to people who will accomplish something with it. Invest in them.

Now, let me drop an even bigger revelation about giving. Every now and then you should give to the person who most dislikes you. Jesus' teaching on this has profound implications:

> *"But love your enemies, and do good, and lend, expecting nothing in return; and your reward will be great, and you will be sons of the Most High; for He Himself is kind to ungrateful and evil men....Give, and it will be given to you;*

91

> *good measure, pressed down, shaken*
> *together, running over, they will pour*
> *into your lap. For by your standard of*
> *measure it shall be measured to you in*
> *return.*"   (Luke 6:35-38)

The latter half of this passage often is taken out of context and used to take offerings; that is OK, but it's really talking about giving to our enemies. If we will give to them, then we will be like God and receive His blessings.

It is difficult to convince some people of this truth, but it is worth trying. Who is it that does not like you? Send them flowers. Buy them a card. Or better yet, send them money as a gift.

When you do this, you will learn more about God's character. *"For by your standard of measure it shall be measured to you in return"* (Luke 6:38b). If you only give to others when you have to, you will live under a tight hand yourself. If, however, you

1. give to your loved ones,
2. bless those who serve you,
3. give away things that weigh you down,
4. give to people who are producing,
5. and give to your enemies,

then you will find an abundant God. He will reveal Himself more clearly to you.

Finally, let us include the poor. Proverbs tells us,

> *He who is generous will be blessed,*
> *For he gives some of his food to the*
> *poor.*   (Prov. 22:9)

A great example is Cornelius who gave many *alms* (money offered to the poor). Cornelius found favor in God's eyes because of his generosity (Acts 10:2).

The Apostle Paul wrote to Timothy and told him to instruct the wealthy among the church to be generous (I Tim. 6:18). Taking those words, I instruct you: Be generous! God likes it. We look not to be paid back by the people to whom we give, but by a God Who is generous and Who already has blessed us (Prov. 19:17). He *is* love and so we must act *in* love.

Ultimately, you will not prosper until you move out of just *earning money* and into *seed planting* and/or *creating wealth*. We explained seed planting in chapter 6. Now let's see the difference between earning money and creating wealth.

Path to Prosperity

earning money ➡ seed planting ➡ creating wealth

Earning money is obvious: you live day by day giving so many hours for so much return. In contrast, if you step into the realm of *creating wealth,* you develop businesses and opportunities for other people. You enter the realm of inventions, new ideas, increased productivity, marketing concepts, implementing plans, etc. Where things were stagnant and there was no money, you develop new opportunities, which attract abundance to flow.

When stepping into creating wealth, you are able to see there is an unlimited amount of money out there, and as you increase in your financial situation, so does everyone associated with you. In contrast, if you earn money, everything that comes into your hands must be taken out of someone else's hand. Therefore, you are dealing with a limited amount of money and as you increase, others decrease.

Creating wealth is better.

Christians should be the most innovative people alive. Look again at our Lord's words in Matthew chapter six. Before telling us to seek the kingdom, Jesus said,

> "Do not lay up for yourselves treasures upon earth, where moth and rust destroy, and where thieves break in and steal. But lay up for yourselves treasures in heaven, where neither moth nor rust destroys, and where thieves do not break in or steal; for where your treasure is, there will your heart be also." (Matt. 6:19-21)

Christians sometime take these verses out of context and talk about not saving money for themselves, but instead, giving it all to God. Some envision a bank account in heaven which will be there upon their arrival because of all they have given during this lifetime. I believe in giving to God by supporting the Church; however, in Matthew 6 that is not what Jesus was teaching. Please read this carefully and see if the following does not make more sense.

Jesus was not telling us about a bank account waiting for us when we get to heaven. That could not be the proper interpretation, because we know that the next life will be filled with treasures, streets of gold, and mansions. We do not need to add our puny treasures to that.

About what, then, was He talking? *Heaven* is a biblical term sometime used to refer to the spiritual dimension or the invisible world around us. Using that definition, where are you to store up treasures? In the spiritual dimension, where moth and rust cannot destroy.

How do you store up these treasures? Jesus explained that your treasure forms wherever your heart is pointed (Matt. 6:21). To understand this, realize your heart is the seat of your faith (Rom. 10:10). Proverbs 4:23 tells us that from the heart flow all the issues of life. As a person directs their heart in a specific direction or toward a goal, the spiritual life within them will build a treasure in the unseen dimension.

This building of a treasure is not to be done independently of God. The context of Matthew 6 is about prayer. Before mentioning spiritual treasure, Jesus taught "The Lord's Prayer" (vs. 6-9). Seven times in verses 1-18, *pay* or *rewards* are mentioned that God gives as a result of our prayer, fasting, almsgiving, and acts of humility. God pays us. He adds to our spiritual treasure. By recognizing that Matthew 6 is about prayer, we can see how we build up a spiritual treasure by spending time with God.

How does this actually work? You have certain needs, desires, and dreams. Do not strive to see those fulfilled. Do not get anxious nor greedy. Do not store up money so you independently can fulfill your goals. Instead, first go to God. Talk to Him. Approach Him as a child, calling Him, "Father." Get your heart clean so He freely can receive you and hear your prayers. Talk to Him about your desires. Pray specifically—in detail. Commit your dreams and plans to God. Partnership with Him.

As you come into agreement with your Partner, faith gradually will fill your heart. Your spiritual reservoir will fill. In time, a sense of dominion will come to you.

This is what it means to seek first His kingdom. Do not try to fulfill your dreams alone. Instead, go to God and seek first to lay up a spiritual treasure. Get the faith first. Enter into God's authority. His kingdom consists of righteousness, peace, and joy (Rom. 14:17); when these qualities fill your heart, that is when you have stepped into the kingdom. That is when God's authority is working with you and the prayer, "Thy kingdom come, Thy will be done," is being answered on your behalf.

Once you have stepped into the kingdom, all things will be added unto you. Opportunities will come your way. Doors will open. You will meet the right people at the right time. Things will fall into place. Provisions will flow into your hands. God will make a way for the fulfillment of your dreams and plans.

As an example, consider a man dreaming about

someday building his own home. As he plans, he is orienting his heart toward that goal. Where his heart is, there will his spiritual treasure be. If he talks to God, faith gradually will grow. As he continues to plan month after month, he will "build that home in the spirit." Confidence will rise in his heart. Finally, one day a sense of dominion will fill him. He will know, "I can do it!" It is at that point that he has found the kingdom, that is, the authority of God, and hence all things will be added unto him.

Likewise, a woman hoping to start a new business will be wise first to plan out every detail. Wherever her heart is pointed, that is where her spiritual treasure will be. Therefore, as she plans, meditates, envisions, and thinks about that new venture, she is forming that business in the spiritual realm. Finally, the day will come when she knows it is time to step out and establish what she already has obtained in the spiritual dimension.

Of course, both Christians and non-Christians can plan and dream in this way, but here is the advantage the Christian has over the non-Christian. God wants to co-partner with you. You have a relationship with Him. As you communicate with God, creative energy will flow. His ideas and desires for your life will be inspired in your mind and heart. As you talk to Him about every detail of your dream, He will breathe life into and shed light upon your plans.

As you partner with God this way, you must embrace the true God, not a false concept of one who is ungiving and unwilling to help you. Jesus instructed us to come before God, calling Him, "Father" (Matt.6:9). Our Lord went on to tell us to look at the birds and lilies (Matt. 6:26-28). See how good God is. Remind yourself of all His blessings. *Fill yourself with an awareness of His greatness.* Walk through nature and embrace the grandeur of the Creator. Your ability to create never will be greater than your concept of God. You never will accomplish more in life than your Source permits. The bigger your dream, the more essential it is that you discover the bigness of the Creator. Partner with that Unlimited One.

You have a dream. You have desires. God wants to help you. Do not think that God is against you, *"...for it is God who is at work in you, both to will and to work for His good pleasure"* (Phil. 2:13). Do you want to start a new business? Do you want to build a new home? Do you want to change your future? It is God rising in you, giving you ideas, causing creative energy to flow. Let that dream mature.

Nurture the dream. Take that dream and put it before God. Talk to Him about it. Plan it. Allow God to inspire every detail within you. Meditate on the things you desire to see fulfilled with Him. Take time—days, weeks, months,—however long it takes—until that dream *takes form in the heavenlies.* Do not store up treasures for yourself on earth where moth and rust can destroy. Instead, seek first the kingdom. Seek the authority of God. Store up for yourself a treasure in the heavenlies.

Now,

Commit your way to the Lord,
Trust also in Him, and He will do it.
(Ps. 37:5)

Come into agreement with Him. Do it together.

This teaching on creative dreaming is no excuse for the person who sits idly in his home merely waiting for "all things to be added to him." Every young man starting out in life needs first to learn how to work 40 hours per week and support himself. Women, too, must live productive lives (I Tim. 5:11-16). Do not be confused concerning what we are teaching in this chapter. We are talking about accessing God's help in our labors.

Allow me to give you some examples of how this works. Consider Orville who owns a restaurant. For several years he just was making a living by selling one meal at a time (earning money). No creativity was evident; he just did the job. But then one day a thriving chain restaurant moved in next door, and Orville knew he would have to change to keep his business going.

So Orville started to dream. At first, no creative ideas came to him. In fact, he simply was discouraged and ready to give up. He had no hope, but then he determined to advance. He believed God did not want him to lose everything. So he got his eyes off of his problems and started reflecting on the goodness of God. He looked at the birds and realized that God takes care of even them. He filled his mind with the greatness of our God. In that frame of mind, inspiration started flowing to him. He knew he could make his business more attractive. In fact, the restaurant next door would be just the thing he needed to make his own restaurant a bigger success. He would specialize, offering unique items that the chain restaurant could not. He would put up an attractive sign and create the image that his restaurant was not just another boring place to eat, but something exciting, wonderful, better than any other place in town. The big restaurant next door would be to his benefit because people would start to identify his area of town as the place to go to eat, but when they got there, he would sweep the customers off the street into his doors.

Understand that a restaurant owner who is just trying to sell meals is *pedaling his tricycle*. On the other hand, a successful owner is trying to *create* an atmosphere where business people can hold an important engagement, or couples can sit for a romantic evening, or friends can come for a memorable experience, or some significant benefit other than food is offered to the people. Where the owner/manager is into creating wealth, an actual energy can be felt in that place. The building regularly is being decorated and the menu improved. Employees are energetic and happy, and customers always leave feeling good.

The restaurant where creative energy is flowing will be a success. That restaurant can charge much more for the same meal that may be served at the restaurant across the street which is prepared by a tricycle pedaler. When creative energy stops, tricycle pedaling must start, and that business will begin dying.

This principle works in every field of employment. The employee simply can go to work and take home a paycheck, or he can spend creative time meditating on how he can improve his productivity, inspire positive attitudes in the whole staff, be a catalyst for everyone else to be more successful, etc. If he wants to be promoted, he needs to invest time in making himself more valuable.

These principles also work in the local church. A pastor may be trying to increase the size of his congregation by adding one more family and holding on tightly (tricycle pedaling). Or he can dream with an unlimited God and fill his ministry with creativity. Perhaps his energy will be toward creating an atmosphere of worship or establishing a community of believers where people of all ages can fellowship. Or maybe he wants the youth to have a powerful drama ministry. Or perhaps God will inspire him to get everyone involved in feeding the poor. The ideas are unlimited, because God is unlimited. The principle, however, is to advance with God, make room in the spiritual dimension, and hence, allow people to be added unto his congregation.

(As I write these words, I am realizing some areas in which I have been trapped personally in tricycle pedaling. I guess I need to spend some time with my Co-partner and hear His ideas.)

As creating, rather than earning, becomes a lifestyle, it answers the problems in every area of life. Included in the creative lifestyle is the whole realm of inventing and solving problems. The person who takes time to solve other people's problems is opening the door for his own advancement. Unfortunately, some people get a great idea, but then take little or no time in dreaming how to market that idea. You must dream through *every* stage of development if you want things to succeed.

Again, we are not talking about *instant* success, nor are we encouraging people to sit around dreaming for the scheme that will end their financial worries. We simply are saying that you must exert creative energy to move into greater success.

Let's conclude this chapter by pointing out the two requirements necessary for creative energy to flow. First, as we have mentioned, you must open yourself to the Unlimited Source. Spend time with Him. Allow yourself to dream freely with Him. Go somewhere you can be relaxed and allow His Spirit to fill you. Think through every detail of what you desire to accomplish. Store up a treasure in the heavenlies. Take a walk with God. Let Him be your Co-partner.

Second, put your heart into your work. The Apostle Paul exhorted Christians, *"Whatever you do, do your work heartily..."* (Col. 3:23). If your whole heart is not in it, creative energy will not flow. Life will be dreary. Tricycle pedaling will become wearisome. If you want to prosper, you must do something you enjoy and enjoy what you do. Remember, your treasure goes where your heart is pointed.

Some Christians wrongly keep their heart away from their work. They think it is unspiritual to enjoy their work. They even feel guilty if they find themselves enjoying natural things too much. They would rather be doing ministry or some "more spiritual" activity. They never have been taught that work is godly and in His plan for our lives. Consequently, they live day by day regretting that they have to be chained to natural responsibilities. Deep in their heart they remain detached from life and all the natural activities surrounding them. They think they are being spiritual, but in reality they are cutting themselves off from the blessings which God wants to bring into their lives.

Don't do that. Embrace life. Enjoy life. Receive it as a blessing from God. Work with your whole heart. Do not feel guilty about enjoying your labors. If you want to prosper, you must put your heart into it. Only then will you move out of earning money and into creating wealth. Come to the place where you can say, "I love work and God is my Partner!"

CHAPTER

10

ACT FROM YOUR GUTS

In the previous chapter we learned about the spiritual reservoir we have. Jesus told us to store up treasures for ourselves, and we learned how to do this through partnering with Him. As our spiritual reservoir becomes established, it opens doors for the fulfillment of that for which we have believed God. As a consequence, all things become added unto us.

The amount of spiritual treasure you presently have exactly equals the sense of dominion in your heart right now—no more, no less. You can feel it in your spirit—right there in your gut! This is the level of your spiritual authority and faith.

The next and final key to prosperity is to act according to the faith you have. For example, if you have been planning and praying for something for a long time and now have a confidence in your heart concerning the accomplishment of that goal, then go ahead and do it—the time is now. God will bless you.

On the other hand, never do anything for which you do not have already a spiritual reservoir. For example, do not go buy a new car unless you have a sense of God's grace when you walk onto the car lot. You may have that sense of dominion without even praying; if you do, it is OK to go ahead. However, you never should start a new business if you do not have an abiding sense of God's blessings. Do not step out to purchase a home until you have a sense of security in your heart. If you do not have confidence and peace, it is not going to work out, no matter how hard you strive to obtain it.

Prosperous people act according to their gut feeling.

I am not talking about your emotions or changing desires. Emotions can lie to you. In fact, when you are emotional and excited about buying something (for example, when a salesman has just given you his sale pitch), it is best to wait until the emotional flare completely dies. And, indeed, it may feel like you are dying inside—that is a good, healthy feeling. If you just have received a large amount of money, you may be tempted to run out and buy something, but that initial excitement may hinder wise decisions. Emotions and desires fluctuate, and hence, they can cloud your awareness of the true level of authority you sense within.

Your gauge needs to be the sense of peace and confidence within. If you will act when that sense of dominion is upon you and within you, God will be there to help you in whatever you are doing.

A good example of this involves dealings I have had with banks. Once while I pastored a church, the congregation and I stepped into a large building project. We raised a lot of money, but we also needed to work with a local bank for their help. I always have tended to be intimidated by bankers. I admit I lack dominion in this area. On this particular occasion I was anxious, even fearful, but knew I needed the banker's help. Before walking into the bank, I got alone with God and meditated on His goodness. I thought about the lilies and how He provides so abundantly. I built up my spiritual reservoir. I reminded myself of God's past goodness to me. Then I walked into the bank with a sense of peace, confidence, even dominion, knowing God was with me. Without much trouble, I got the help we needed.

Later while trying to complete the building project, we came to a crisis point where we could not pay our bills. This time I ran to the bank in a state of anxiety. I tried not to let it show, but somehow the spiritual dynamics were at work and the banker would not even consider my proposal.

I knew where I had failed and so again I got alone with God. I stayed with Him until peace and confidence came over my being. This time I did not even have to go to the bank, but the money came almost supernaturally through church members.

If you have an area in your life where you just cannot get the victory, then trust someone who does have a sense of dominion in that area. Because I always have struggled in dealing with banks, I have learned to trust my wife in that area. She is incredibly relaxed in that environment, and I have seen things go in her favor every time she deals with a bank. When she walks into our local bank, she smiles and waves to most of the officers as if she were walking through the living room of our own home. One time I had prepared my financial reports perfectly and did everything naturally oriented in order to establish a line of credit for our publishing department. I was turned down. Later my wife walked into the same bank in a totally disorganized fashion to settle another matter. In fact, she carried all her financial records in a laundry basket and plopped them down in front of the bank president. Before she was through, she was laughing with everyone around and had obtained everything she had sought.

I am not telling you to be disorganized. No. I am telling you that confidence and peace are more important, and if you do not have them, then depend on someone who already has dominion in your weak areas.

If you are anxious about buying a car, then find someone with a relaxed attitude about it to shop for you. If you need a new job, but really do not believe that God will give you a good one, then submit yourself to the authority of another person, such as an employment seeker who does have a relaxed, confident attitude about finding you work. If you are not good at selling things, then let someone who is good at it sell what you want to turn into cash.

It is foolish for you to try to accomplish things in areas for which you do not have a sense of dominion. There is a spiritual reservoir. If you do not have enough in your reservoir to accomplish some specific task, don't try it—not yet, anyway.

As we stated earlier, prosperous people do what they sense inside is right. They do what they know they can handle confidently.

King David wrote his confession to God,

> *Oh Lord, my heart is not proud, nor my*
> *eyes haughty;*
> *Nor do I involve myself in great matters,*
> *Or in things too difficult for me.*
> *Surely I have quieted and composed my*
> *soul....* (Ps. 131:1-2)

Notice the progression of thoughts in these verses. The pride of life and the lust of the eyes can cause people to get involved in things too big for them. In pointing this out, we are not telling people never to do anything great. On the contrary, King David ruled a whole nation, but he knew it was not too difficult for him. He could handle it. In the midst of all his responsibilities, he still could quiet his soul and stay composed.

Poverty-minded people are not composed. They are anxious. Or they become obsessed with the task before them. They try to do too much or not enough. They involve themselves in things much too early or too big for themselves, and hence, lose much—again and again.

An excellent gauge of one's present level of authority is whatever they can handle without bragging about it. This is *key*. If a poverty-minded person wins a million dollars, he will be over-whelmed and have to show it off somehow. He will

111

not be composed, but he will yield to the pride of life. It is OK for a person to have emotional excitement, but when they "have to" draw attention to themselves, it is because they are enjoying something beyond their present level of authority, and in a short time they will lose it.

If a person receives something that is within their already-established level of authority, it will be "no big deal" to them. They may be happy about it. They may share their joy with another person. However, they will not be *compelled* to tell others about it.

This applies to all areas of life. If you buy a car that is so nice you are bursting with pride, you very likely may get in a wreck. If you receive an inheritance that overwhelms you, there will be forces at work to cause you to lose it in time. If you are offered a job that pays so much you lose your composure, you will not keep that job very long. If you gain anything without first growing into it, you will not keep it. This is life.

Prosperous people are aware of these truths. When considering what to entrust to their children, they know what their children will be able to handle. When watching friends and relatives, they sense the level of authority in the hearts of each. They know what they themselves can handle, and, as King David, they do not involve themselves in great matters nor in things too difficult for them (Ps. 131:1).

May God grant you the prosperous sense to not get yourself in over your head.

Often Christians misunderstand the biblical definition of faith and, hence, try to violate these truths. For example, some Christians with a wrong concept of faith think that faith makes a person reach above their present level of authority. That is false. Faith is a condition of the heart (Rom. 10:10). It comes with an inner sense of confidence and peace. When a person has faith, they act, possess, accomplish, and advance. To go beyond one's present level of faith is presumption. It is grasping at chance, not God, and it will not produce lasting benefits. True faith does move mountains, but the mountains first are moved in the heart.

We have taught you how to raise your level of authority and increase your faith. You are not stuck at the level where you presently find yourself. You can change. Throughout this book, we have been showing you how to cultivate a prosperous soul. Unless you change the inside, you never will change the outside for any length of time.

Allow me to draw a final lesson here from the professional gambler. Some of my Christian readers may object at this point, wondering why I ever would refer to such questionable practices. Please do not take this wrongly. I am not encouraging gambling in any way, but I want to teach a principle here.

No successful professional gambler ever gambles. Try to understand this. When we talk about gambling here, we are talking about a person who tries to make money by taking chances. Professional gamblers never do that. They are too smart for that. A professional gambler once passed on his secret: "I never allow myself to be put into a position where I can't afford to lose." Think about this. A professional gambler never allows himself to be put into a position where, if he lost, he would be devastated. Why? Because if he allowed himself to be put into that position, he would lose his sense of confidence and peace. He would lose his ability to think, calculate the odds, and make wise decisions. He cannot allow himself to be there. Successful, professional gamblers really are not gambling. They are playing wisely and figuring the odds to work in their favor. They are investing, not gambling, and because they keep a sense of dominion every minute, the odds tend to go their way more often.

Remember, to some degree a sense of dominion produces abundance both for the Christian and the non-Christian. We discussed the advantages which the Christian has. What is tragic is when the Christian does not take advantage of the very principles laid out by our Lord Jesus.

Don't take chances. Don't gamble. To do anything beyond what you have the confidence to do is gambling. It is trusting in chance. It is not faith. It is foolishness. From this day forward only do what feels right—not in your emotions, but right in your gut.

Conclusion

Sooner or later you must get off of your tricycle (earning-money mentality) and travel by faster means. This is not an excuse to quit your present job. Be a realist. You have to pay your bills. You need to work hard. However, as you continue down life's road, advance into better areas of employment. At the same time, start planting seeds and allowing the creative energy of God to flow through you.

Do not slip into the delusion that you will get rich overnight! Instead, expect to move into a prosperous lifestyle gradually.

Think long-range. Make a five-year plan. Today you can start changing your thought patterns. Read this book several times—until it's a part of your thinking patterns. Determine that by this time next year you will have conquered the poverty spirit. Believe that prosperity will be flowing from God into your life. As a result, three years from today you will be living a different lifestyle. You will be on top, the stress of bills gone, some amount being invested, and creative energy flowing. Five years from today, expect the harvest of your seed planting to start overtaking you. By the end of your life, believe that you will have lived out your dreams.

It is a lifestyle—continually advancing. You can have an abundance to accomplish on earth what God put you here to do. You can help others succeed. This is the will of God for your life.

THE COMPLETE WINESKIN (Fourth edition)

The Body of Christ is in a reformation. God is pouring out the Holy Spirit and our wineskins must be changed to handle the new wine. Will the Church come together in unity? Where do small group meetings fit? How does the anointing of God work and what is your role? What is the 5-fold ministry? How are apostles, prophets, evangelists, pastors and teachers going to rise up and work together? This book puts into words what you have been sensing in your spirit. (Eberle's best seller, translated into many languages, distributed worldwide.)

TWO BECOME ONE

Releasing God's Power for Romance, Sexual Freedom and Blessings in Marriage

Kindle afresh the "buzz of love." Find out how to make God's law of binding forces work for you instead of against you. The keys to a thrilling, passionate, and fulfilling marriage can be yours if you want them. This book is of great benefit to pastors, counselors, young singles, divorcees and especially married people. Couples are encouraged to read it together.

THE LIVING SWORD

"The truth shall set you free." So then why does Christian fight Christian over doctrinal issues that seem so clear to each side? Can both be right, or wrong? Learn how Jesus used the Scriptures in His day and then apply those principles to controversial issues currently facing us such as women in the ministry, divorce and remarriage, prosperity, God's plan for our lives,.... What we need is the leading of the Holy Spirit on these subjects. This book will bring the Scriptures alive and set you free.

GOD'S LEADERS FOR TOMORROW'S WORLD

(Revised/expanded edition) You sense a call to leadership in your life, but questions persist: "Does God want me to rise up? Is this pride? Do I truly know where to lead? How can I influence people?" Through a new understanding of leadership dynamics, learn how to develop godly charisma. Confusion will melt into order when you see the God-ordained lines of authority. Fear of leadership will change to confidence as you learn to handle power struggles. Move into your "metron," that is, your God-given authority. You can be all God created you to be!

DEVELOPING A PROSPEROUS SOUL
VOL I: HOW TO OVERCOME A POVERTY MIND-SET
VOL II: HOW TO MOVE INTO GOD'S FINANCIAL BLESSINGS

There are fundamental changes you can make in the way you think which will release God's blessings. This is a balanced look at the promises of God with practical steps you can take to move into financial freedom. It is time for Christians to recapture the financial arena.

SPIRITUAL REALITIES

Here they are—the series explaining how the spiritual world and the natural world relate. In this series Harold R. Eberle deals with issues such as:

- What exists in the spiritual world
- Discerning things in the spirit
- Interpretation of dreams
- Angelic and demonic visitations
- How people access the spiritual realm
- Out-of-body experiences
- What the dead are experiencing
- Christian perspective of holistic medicine
- Activities of witches, psychics and New Agers
- Spiritual impartations and influences between people
- Science and the Bible including creation, life on other planets, quantum mechanics,...
- Understanding supernatural phenomena from a biblical perspective

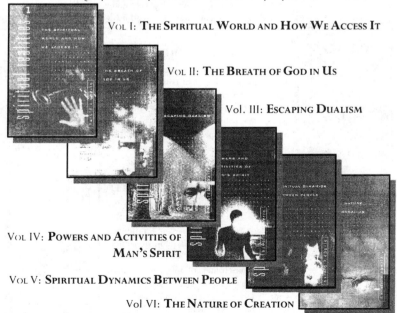

VOL I: THE SPIRITUAL WORLD AND HOW WE ACCESS IT

VOL II: THE BREATH OF GOD IN US

Vol. III: ESCAPING DUALISM

VOL IV: POWERS AND ACTIVITIES OF MAN'S SPIRIT

VOL V: SPIRITUAL DYNAMICS BETWEEN PEOPLE

Vol VI: THE NATURE OF CREATION

PRECIOUS IN HIS SIGHT *A Fresh Look at the Nature of Man*
During the Fourth Century Augustine taught about the nature of man using as his key Scripture a verse in the book of Romans which had been mistranslated. Since that time the Church has embraced a false concept of man which has negatively influenced every area of Christianity. It is time for Christians to come out of darkness! This book, considered by many to be Harold Eberle's greatest work, has implications upon our understanding of sin, salvation, Who God is, evangelism, the world around us and how we can live the daily, victorious lifestyle.

YOU SHALL RECEIVE POWER
Moving Beyond Pentecostal & Charismatic Theology
God's Spirit will fill you in measures beyond what you are experiencing presently. This is not just about Pentecostal or Charismatic blessings. There is something greater. It is for all Christians, and it will build a bridge between those Christians who speak in tongues and those who do not. It is time for the whole Church to take a fresh look at the work of the Holy Spirit in our individual lives. This book will help you. It will challenge you, broaden your perspective, set you rejoicing, fill you with hope, and leave you longing for more of God.

DEAR PASTORS AND TRAVELING MINISTERS,
Here is a manual to help pastors and traveling ministers relate and minister together effectively. Topics are addressed such as ethical concerns, finances, authority, scheduling,.... In addition to dealing with real-life situations, an appendix is included with very practical worksheets to offer traveling ministers and local pastors a means to communicate with each other. Pastors and traveling ministers can make their lives and work much easier by using this simple, yet enlightening, manual.

To place an order or to check current prices call:
1-800-308-5837 within the USA or:
509-248-5837 from outside the USA
(MasterCard/Visa accepted)

Winepress Publishing
P.O. Box 10653, Yakima, WA 98909-1653, USA

E-mail: winepress@nwinfo.net
Web Site: www.winepress.org
Some books available as an audiobook on cassette tapes.